SPANISH FOOTBALL FEDERATION
COACHING PROGRAM U9-12

Written by
EDUARDO VALCÁRCEL

Fundación RFEF

Published by

SPANISH FOOTBALL FEDERATION COACHING PROGRAM U9-12

First Published February 2018 by SoccerTutor.com

Info@soccertutor.com | www.SoccerTutor.com
UK: 0208 1234 007 | **US:** (305) 767 4443 | **ROTW:** +44 208 1234 007

ISBN: 978-1-910491-17-1

Copyright: SoccerTutor.com Limited © 2018. All Rights Reserved.

All rights reserved. No part of this publication may be reproduced, stored in a retrieval system, or transmitted in any form or by any means, electronic, mechanical, photocopy, recording or otherwise, without prior written permission of the copyright owner. Nor can it be circulated in any form of binding or cover other than that in which it is published and without similar condition including this condition being imposed on a subsequent purchaser.

Author
Eduardo Valcárcel

Original Spanish Publishers
Abfutbol ©, All Rights Reserved.

Edited by
Alex Fitzgerald - SoccerTutor.com

Cover Design by
Alex Macrides, Think Out Of The Box Ltd.
Email: design@thinkootb.com Tel: +44 (0) 208 144 3550

Diagrams
Diagram designs by SoccerTutor.com. All the diagrams in this book have been created using SoccerTutor.com Tactics Manager Software available from www.SoccerTutor.com

Note: While every effort has been made to ensure the technical accuracy of the content of this book, neither the author nor publishers can accept any responsibility for any injury or loss sustained as a result of the use of this material.

"IN THIS LIFE, IF YOU WANT SOMETHING, WITH A DREAM, SACRIFICE AND DISCIPLINE, YOU CAN GET IT"

Eduardo Valcárcel

CONTENTS

Foreword by Vicente Del Bosque 8
The Spanish Football Federation Coaching School 9
The Coaching Program 10
Coaching Tips to Consider 11
Diagram Key 13
Practice Format 13

CHAPTER 1: RUNNING WITH THE BALL AT SPEED 14
RUNNING WITH THE BALL AT SPEED TRAINING METHODOLOGY 15
RWTB at Speed with Changes of Direction Circuit 16
RWTB at Speed into Different Positions in the 3-3-1 Formation 17
RWTB at Speed in a 3 Team Race Circuit 18
Speed and Technique 1 v 1 Race 19
Quick Reactions in a RWTB at Speed Competition 20
Quick Decision Making & RWTB at Speed in Different Situations 21
RWTB at Speed into a Guarded Central Square 22
RWTB at Speed to Lose a Marker (Shadowing in Pairs) 23
RWTB at Speed "Collect the Treasure Game" 24

CHAPTER 2: DRIBBLING PAST OPPONENTS & 1 V 1 DUELS 25
DRIBBLING PAST OPPONENTS TRAINING METHODOLOGY 26
Moves to Beat Defenders in a Continuous Cycle 27
Dribbling to Beat an Opponent in a Zonal 1 v 1 Duel 28
Dribbling to Beat an Opponent in an End to End Practice 29
Dribbling Past Opponents "Bulldog Game" 30
Dribbling Past Opponents and Keeping the Ball "One Minute Game" ... 31
Dribbling Past Opponents & Through Cone Gates in 1 v 1 Situations ... 32
Sprint, Change Direction, Receive, Beat Opponent + Finish 33
Quick Reactions and Dribbling Past Opponents in 1 v 1 Duels 34

CHAPTER 3: DUELS (2 V 1, 2 V 2, 3 V 1, 3 V 2, 3 V 3) 35
DUELS TRAINING METHODOLOGY 36
Lose Marker, Receive and Pass Back 37
Quick Attack in a 2 v 1 (+1 Supporting Player) Duel 38

Dribbling and Shooting with 2 v 1 Duel 39
One-Two, Receive and 2 v 1 Duel 40
2 v 2 (+1) Duel Game with 4 Goals 41
Consecutive 2 v 1 Duels with Attackers Split into 2 Side Channels 42
Awareness, Quick Reactions to Receive and 2 v 2 Duels 43
Fast Attack in a 3 v 2 Duel 44
1 v 1 Duels into Collective 3 v 2 Duel 45
Continuous 2 (+2) v 2 Duels with Two Goals 46
Continuous 3 v 3 Duel Team Game 47

CHAPTER 4: PASSING 49

PASSING TRAINING METHODOLOGY 50

Dribble + One-Two in a Passing Square 51
Free Passing in Pairs Against Restricted Defenders 52
Passing in Continuous 2 v 1 Situations 53
One-Two Passing Combinations at Different Angles 54
'Y Shape' Passing Practice with One-Two Combinations 55
Short and Long Passing in a Double Square Practice 56
Quick One-Two, Pass & Follow in a Double Square Practice 57
One-Two on the Outside, Pass and Supporting Run on the Inside 58
Building Up Play to Pass and Switch Play in a 1 v 1 Channel Game 59
Passing Forward in a 3 Zone Small Sided Game 60

CHAPTER 5: RONDOS 61

RONDOS TRAINING METHODOLOGY 62

5 v 1 Rondo with 2 Balls (1 with Feet, 1 with Hands) 63
5 v 2 Rondo with Movement to Switch Sides 64
4 (+1) v 2 Rondo with Inside Player Switching with Outside Players 65
5 v 2 Rondo "Hit the Middle Cone" 66
4 v 2 Rondos and Speed Exercises 67
Changing 4 v 1 Rondo Positions with Support Play in 4 Squares 68
Transition from Attack to Defence in Simultaneous 4 v 1 Rondos 69
End to End 4 (+3) v 4 Rondo 70

CHAPTER 6: POSSESSION GAMES 71

POSSESSION TRAINING METHODOLOGY 72

Possession Game with Increasing Opposition (5 v 1 to 5 v 5) 73
Three Team 4 (+4) v 4 Possession Game 74
Support Play in an 8 v 6 Possession Game 75

Possession Game with Players Switching Inside / Outside 76
Three Team Possession Game with Receiving Corners 77
Possession Play in a 2 Zone Transition Game 78
Retain the Ball and Switch Play in a Two Sided Possession Game 79
Possession and Switching Play in a Three Team Zonal Game 80
Possession Game with Quick Reaction Sprints...................................... 81

CHAPTER 7: HEADING 82

HEADING TRAINING METHODOLOGY 83
Headed Pass + Compete in the Air in a Continuous Circuit Warm Up 84
'Score Only with Headers' in a 7 v 7 Warm Up Game 85
Backwards Headers Relay Race 86
Consecutive Header Team Game 87
Competing for Headers at Different Angles and Heights............................ 88
Resistance, Sprint + Headed Finish.. 89
Hand + Header Game / Sprint, Hurdle + Header / Chip + Header................... 90
Sprint + Headed Finish / 3 v 3 Hands and Headers Game 91
Headed Passes and Quick Break Away with Finish 92
Connected 2 Zone Duels with Headers + Counter Attacks 93
Hands + Headers Small Sided Game with Delivery from Wide Players 94

CHAPTER 8: FINISHING 95

FINISHING TRAINING METHODOLOGY 96
Dribble / Sprint Exercises + Finishing 97
Dribbling Exercises + Combined Finishing 98
Ball Over Head: Spin, Control, Dribble + Shoot 99
One-Two, Open Up, Receive + Shoot... 100
Drop, Turn, Receive + Finish 101
Sprint, Turn, Receive + Shoot in a Three Player Combination 102
Quick Combination, Supporting Run from Wide + Finish 103
Double One-Two and Finishing Practice 104
Short and Long Passing with Finishing from Cut Backs 105
Finishing in a 3 v 3 SSG with 2 Extra Attacking Outside Players................... 106

CHAPTER 9: ATTACKING COMBINATION PLAY.......................... 107

ATTACKING COMBINATION PLAY TRAINING METHODOLOGY 108
Quick One Touch Pass and Move Combination Practice........................... 109
Two Mirrored One Touch Combinations + Finishing 110
Quick Combination Play with Different Supporting Runs + Finishing............... 111

Flank Play, Supporting Runs and Finishing 112
Pass High Up the Flank, Supporting Runs + Finishing.. 113
Quick Combination Play to Receive High Up on Flank, Cross + Finish....................... 114
Quick Combination Play with Inside Movement to Receive + Shoot 115
Quick Combination Play with Fast Support, Cross + Finish 116
Combination Play to Receive on the Flank, Cross + Finish.................................... 117
Win the Ball (2 v 4) in the Centre and Counter Attack Combination.......................... 118

CHAPTER 10: TACTICAL DEVELOPMENT 119
TACTICAL DEVELOPMENT TRAINING METHODOLOGY..................................... 120
Build Up to Finish in an 8 v 2 Zonal Game 121
Build Up to Finish in an 8 v 3 Zonal Game + Quick Transition................................. 122
Build Up to Finish in an 8 v 4 Zonal Game 123
Build Up to Finish in an 8 v 8 Zonal Game with Restricted Defenders 124
Build Up to Finish in an 8 v 8 Small Sided Game 125

CHAPTER 11: CIRCUITS 127
CIRCUIT TRAINING METHODOLOGY.. 128
Dribbling Circuit with Different Techniques and Turns 129
2 v 2 Possession Game + Speed & Agility Exercises with Finishing 130
Speed & Agility Circuit Training with Finishing (3 v 1 Attack) 131
Speed & Agility Circuit Training with 3 v 2 Duel... 132

FOREWORD BY VICENTE DEL BOSQUE

COACHING ROLES

- Spain (2008 - 2016)
- Beşiktaş (2004 - 2005)
- Real Madrid (1999 - 2003)

HONOURS

- FIFA World Cup (2010)
- UEFA European Championship (2012)
- UEFA Champions League (2000, 2002)
- La Liga (2001, 2003)
- FIFA World Coach of the Year (2012)
- UEFA Club Coach of the Year (2002)
- Top 10 Greatest Coaches of UEFA era (1954—2016)
- 5 La Liga titles & 4 Copa Del Rey titles as a player for Real Madrid
- 18 Spain caps

"A school beyond sport"

I think this book can be considered a prize for the years of work done by professionals working in the Football Schools of the RFEF (Spanish Football Federation). All of them are very good coaches, but what is more important in my point of view, is that they are great educators.

I have the opportunity to see the work that is done with the children in the schools of the RFEF live. I am proud to observe the treatment of the students. As well as teaching them all the technical skills they need and how to position themselves on the pitch, they are instilled in the values of fellowship, teamwork, discipline, and respect for their coach, teammates and opponents.

For me this part is fundamental, because in the end it is what is left for life, beyond that when they become adults, they may become professional football players or they may not. What they are sure to be is people and thanks to the efforts of my colleagues it seems that they are going to become great people. They are provided with the "tools" to achieve this.

I really wish this book to become a great success as it undoubtedly reflects the enthusiasm, professionalism and high level of training our coaches have at the RFEF.

THE SPANISH FOOTBALL FEDERATION COACHING SCHOOL

"In the School of the RFEF, we form sportsmen with values."

Eduardo Valcárcel (2017) **- Director of the Spanish Football Federation Coaching School** (Real Federación Española de Fútbol, RFEF)

As Director of the School of the Spanish Football Federation, Eduardo Valcárcel had to take stock of the latest season. The following is from July 2017.

It has been a year in which we continue our progress, always based on the principles of discipline, solidarity, education and respect to the referees.

Principles: The key is consistency and we must remind coaches, because we are all human and we all like to win but before seeking a victory, we must think about creating athletes with values, rather than just players.

Progression: We started with 70 children 9 years ago and today we have 850. We started with 4 coaches and today we are 40.

It was a modest idea in 2008 and today we are a benchmark throughout Spain because not only everybody knows us, but we are recognised and respected for the job that we do."

The Future: We go year after year. One of the keys to everything going well is that we do not think of distant dreams, but we work in the day to day, driven by the values with which we have grown.

THE COACHING PROGRAM

EDUARDO VALCÁRCEL
Director RFEF Coaching

I am the **Director of the School of the Real Federación Española de Fútbol (Spanish Football Federation)**. For many years, I have had the great dream of creating a book to include all of our football practices we use at the Spanish Football Federation. It has not been an easy task, because in it I wanted to capture the work of many coaches who, with love and dedication, give every day, so that the children can progress and learn in the best way possible.

The Football School of the Spanish Federation currently has more than 800 students aged between 4 and 15 years old. We take into account the application of the methodology of learning by age, so that the child ends up being an athlete and a professional football player.

In the book, the practices displayed are performed by children in the U9-12 level. By increasing the difficulty or simply the speed of execution, these same practices are applicable to the next age bracket, since they are complete and very useful for the improvement of all football players.

Throughout the season, we practice these exact types of activities, because we consider it fundamental that the children learn and understand the practices perfectly, and little by little, work on variations that make them more difficult, forcing them to strive for the perfect execution.

I still remember when I started to coach 26 years ago and performed the practices with great enthusiasm, I put in everything using my maximum energy, I thought at that time that everything I did was good. However, now I realise after years of experience, how much I have learned and am now able to apply to be a better coach.

One hundred percent of the work done today, is undoubtedly one of the great and most profitable changes of all these years in football. Developing players need to train while always using the ball - with it the work will always be much better and more fruitful. This is my best advice, to always have players using a ball in your sessions from beginning to end, for all practices.

COACHING TIPS TO CONSIDER

To start this book, I would like to offer a series of tips for new coaches, the results of the experience accumulated during many years of work.

1. First of all, we must exclude practices where players are waiting in queues. And if they do have to exist, there is a minimal wait, otherwise we have reduced practice time for our players. Try to change the queue concept to that of **ONE CHILD, ONE BALL**.

2. An alternative to avoid players queueing, is to have two or three practices at the same time whenever possible, something that we must do often if we are lucky enough to have an assistant coach with sufficient material. In this way, by dividing the work, we can better help the players and reach them more often, achieving our session goals in a shorter time and therefore having more time for other types of practices.

3. Take care of the details in everything you do and not to plan during the session, plan everything before. This way the practices are seen and understood much better when you have collected everything, referring to previous experience. This way you can appreciate (in a cleaner way) the activities to be performed.

4. Do not allow insults or disrespect between players or members of the coaching staff, as in the long term this weakens the group and creates cracks which are difficult to close later.

5. When explaining a practice to the players, remember to do it in a brief and concise way, so as not to bore the players and thus delay the start of the task. You should also take care of your gestural attitude, which together with the tone of voice you use, become key for the progression and attitude of the child.

6. Whenever possible, we must work on the basis of the game system and therefore have it as a reference in our practices in relation to possession, combination play and tactical development, for example.

7. When we perform possession practices with equal sized teams, depending on the level of the players, it can be difficult to chain three, four or five passes in a row, so we must force the defenders to play while holding hands. In this way we improve the confidence of the ball carrier and it gives the players a few more seconds to execute the 'receive + pass' technical action.

DIAGRAM KEY

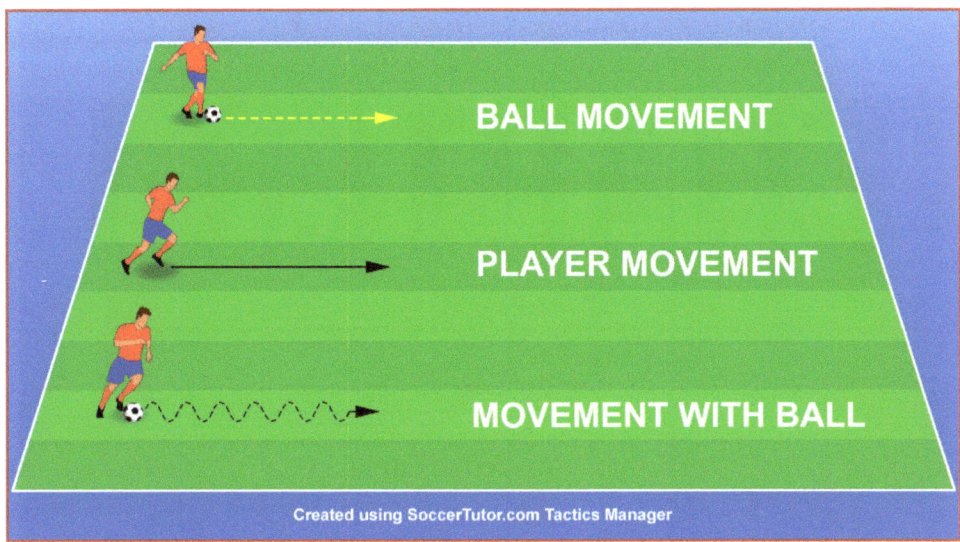

PRACTICE FORMAT

Each practice includes clear diagrams with supporting training notes such as:

- Name of Practice
- Objective of Practice
- Description of Practice
- Variations or Progressions (if applicable)

CHAPTER 1

Running with the Ball at Speed

RUNNING WITH THE BALL AT SPEED TRAINING METHODOLOGY

- The best part of the foot to use to run with the ball at speed should always be the outer instep (laces).

- The other parts of the foot slow the speed at which a player can run with the ball, but they allow greater control.

- The aim is for players to develop great control of the ball when running at speed with both the left and right foot.

- When a player becomes equally comfortable running with the ball with both feet, they will develop absolute control with the ball in motion - they will be able to run at full speed, change direction, turn etc.

- The next step is decision making. The players learn to run with the ball at speed when there is not a good forward passing option and there is space ahead to run into without opposition.

Chapter 1: Running with the Ball at Speed

RWTB at Speed with Changes of Direction Circuit

4 x 2 min

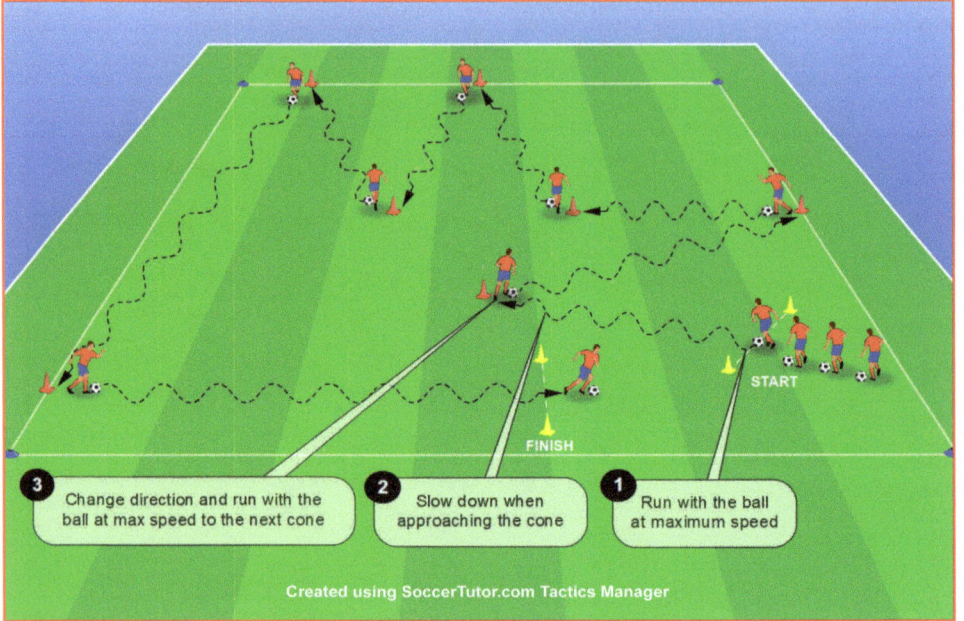

Objective: Running with the ball at maximum speed, slowing down and changing direction.

Description

Within a 25 x 25 yard area, we mark out cones in the positions shown. In this practice we have 12 players all with a ball, 7 of which start on the red cones as shown. The other players all start from in between the yellow starting cone gate.

The players must:

1. Run with the ball at maximum speed towards the next cone.
2. Slow down when they approach the cone.
3. Finally, change direction to run with the ball at maximum speed to the next cone.

This is repeated until they reach the finish line. The players perform continuous circuits for 2 minutes before having a rest. Repeat this 4 times.

Variation

On the signal of the coach, all the players must change direction - the finish line becomes the start line and vice versa.

Chapter 1: Running with the Ball at Speed

RWTB at Speed into Different Positions in the 3-3-1 Formation

8 min

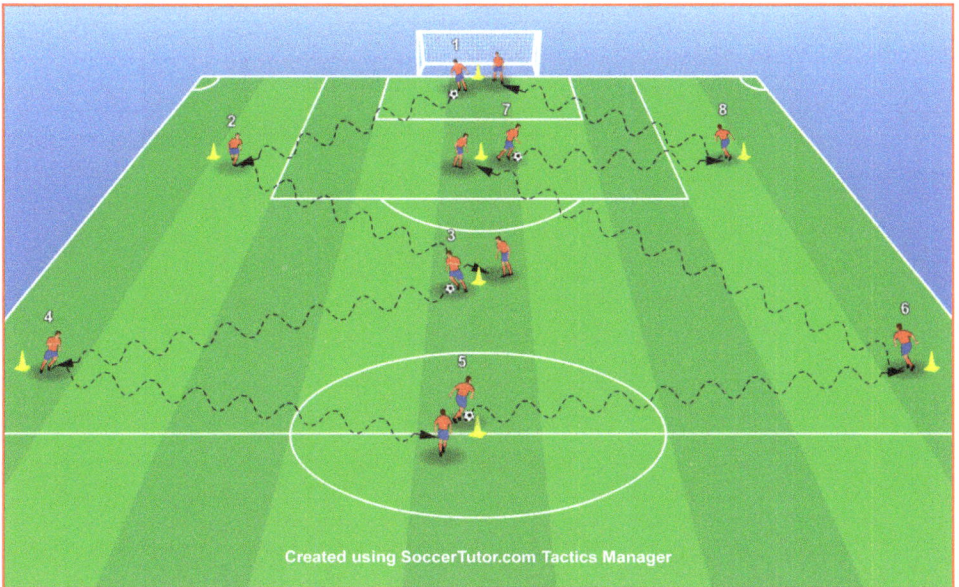

Objective: Running with the ball at speed, to and from different positions on the pitch.

Description

For this practice, we have 12 players within half a youth pitch.

The cones are set out to replicate the 3-3-1 formation we use for an 8 v 8 competitive games. There are 2 players on each central cone and 1 player on each wide cone.

We start with 4 balls at the same time from the central cones (1, 3, 5 & 7). The players run with the ball to the next cone where they give the ball to the next player. They stay on that cone waiting for the next player and ball to arrive.

This practice is a continuous circuit (1 -> 2 -> 3 -> 4 -> 5 -> 6 -> 7 -> Start).

Variations

1. Create a different sequence with the possibility of changing direction after a signal from the coach.
2. Include a pass or two as part of the sequence.

Chapter 1: Running with the Ball at Speed

RWTB at Speed in a 3 Team Race Circuit

4 x 3 min

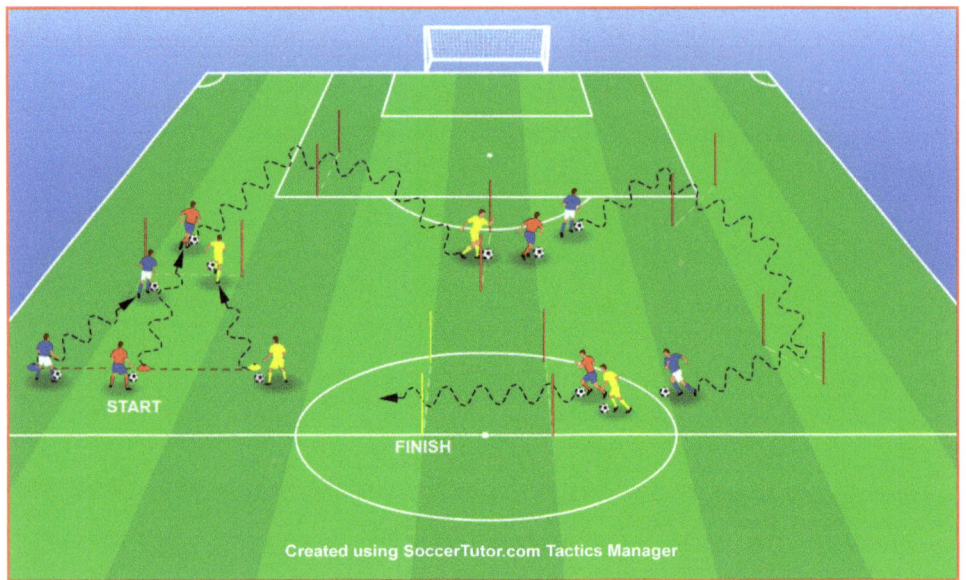

Objective: Ball mastery with different parts of the foot and running with the ball at speed in a competitive race.

Description

Using half a youth pitch, we mark out 7 pole gates in the positions shown. The players are in three teams and every player has a ball.

One player from each team starts running with the ball around the circuit as quickly as they can. If a pole gate is missed, the player must go back and go through it.

The first player to cross the finish line scores 1 point for their team. Multiple groups can race at the same time as shown - just leave enough time in between the groups.

The players do 4 repetitions of 3 minutes. The team with the most points at the end wins.

Variation

Perform it as a relay with players standing at different stages of the circuit, waiting for their teammate and taking the ball from them to continue the race.

Progression

The players have to complete the circuit running with 2 balls at their feet.

Chapter 1: Running with the Ball at Speed

Speed and Technique 1 v 1 Race

8-10 min

Objective: Ball mastery, running with the ball and reaction speed.

Description

Mark out a square appropriate for the level of the players. We position lines of 4 cones and a small pole gate (or mini goals) in each corner, as shown in the diagram.

For this practice, there are 2 players waiting by the central cone with a ball. They wait for the coach to call out 2 colours.

As soon as the coach calls out 2 colours (e.g. "Yellow or Blue"), the players must dribble the ball towards the corner of one of those colours, slalom through the 4 cones and then pass the ball in between the poles (or mini goals) to score.

Only the player who scores first gets a point.

Variations

1. Call out 1 colour and the players compete to try and score in the same goal.
2. Have 4 players and call out 2 colours.
3. Have 4 players who race to complete all 4 corners consecutively.

Quick Reactions in a RWTB at Speed Competition

8-10 min

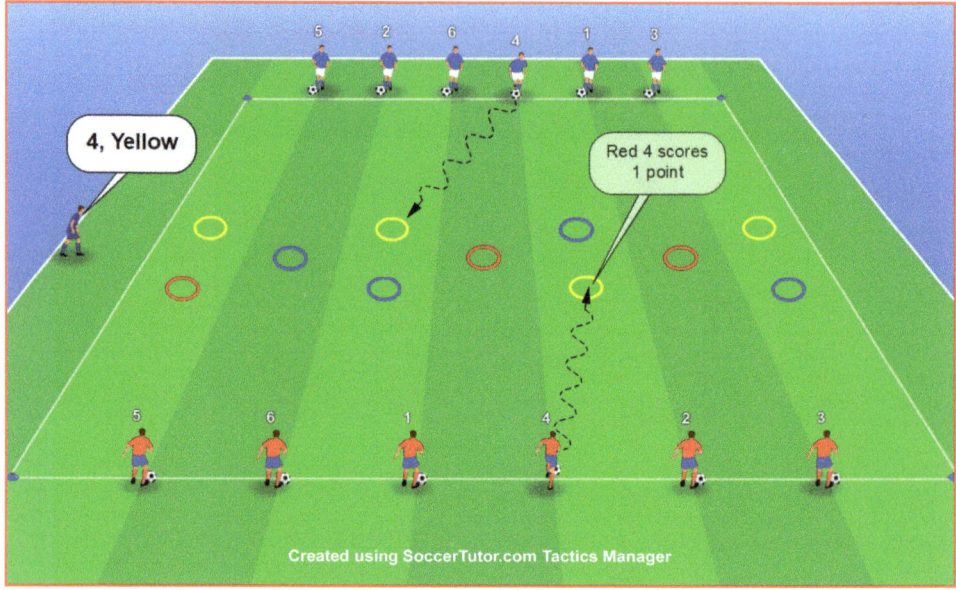

Objective: Quick reactions and running with the ball at speed from a standing start.

Description

We mark out a 20 x 20 yard square and place different coloured hoops in the centre as shown. We have two teams of 6 players, each assigned a different number.

The practice starts when the coach calls out a number and a colour.

In the diagram example, No.4 from the red and blue teams must react quickly and dribble the ball into a yellow hoop. The first player to do this scores a point for their team.

Variations

1. The coach calls out several numbers and 1 colour.
2. The coach calls out 1 number and several colours. The players then have to dribble and stop the ball in all the coloured hoops consecutively, in the order the coach calls them out.
3. The coach calls out several numbers and several colours.

Chapter 1: Running with the Ball at Speed

Quick Decision Making & RWTB at Speed in Different Situations

8-10 min

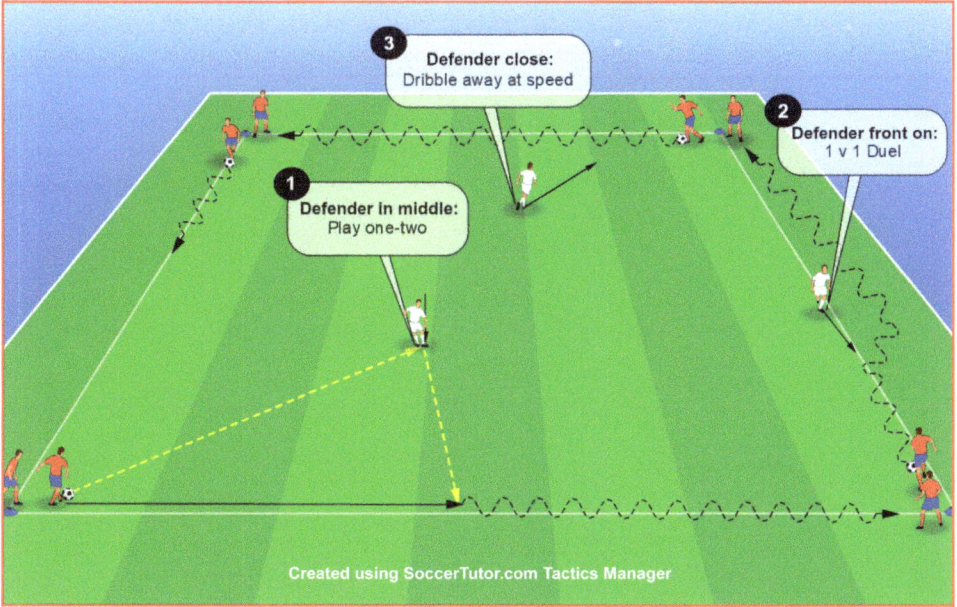

Objective: We work on decision making when presented with different situations - whether to pass, dribble front on in a 1 v 1 duel or dribble with speed into space.

Description

Mark out a 15-20 yard square. We have 8 red attacking players (2 in each corner) and 3 white defenders inside.

The practice starts with 4 players (each with a ball) simultaneously from each corner. They must look up at the position of the defender so that they can make the right decision, before dribbling the ball to the next player at the next corner:

1. If the defender is positioned towards the middle, the player plays a one-two with the defender, receives back and dribbles to the next corner.
2. If the defender is front on, then dribble forward and try to beat him in a 1 v 1 duel.
3. If the defender is close and to the side, dribble forward into the space at speed.

The defenders change corners after each action.

Progressions

1. On the signal of the coach, all the players must change direction.
2. Change how they receive - move off cone before receiving a pass from a teammate.

Spanish Football Federation Coaching

Chapter 1: Running with the Ball at Speed

RWTB at Speed into a Guarded Central Square

8 min

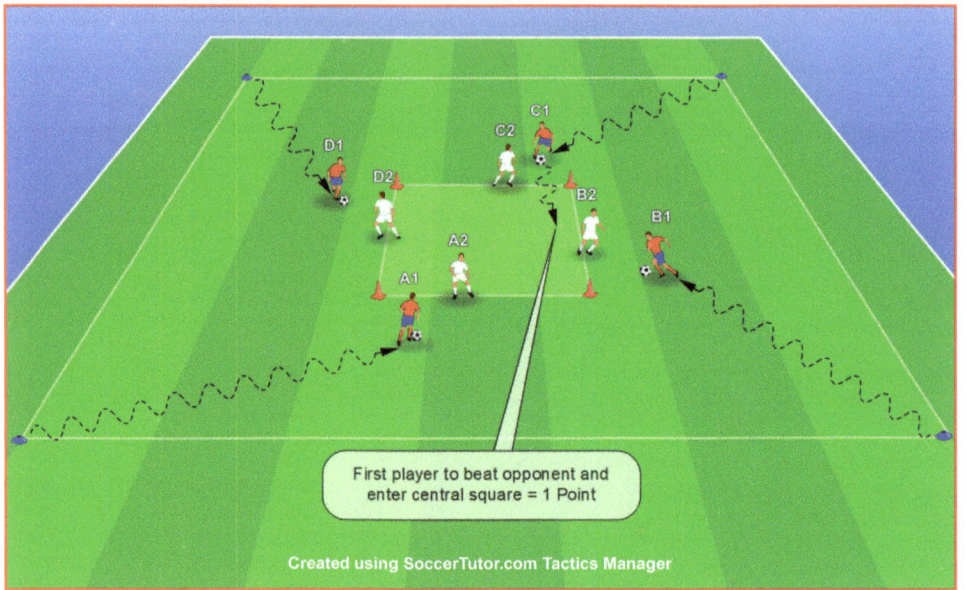

First player to beat opponent and enter central square = 1 Point

Objective: Running with the ball at speed accurately and past an opponent.

Description

In a 20 x 20 yard area we mark out a 5 x 5 yard central square. We have 8 players in pairs - 4 players (reds) start with a ball in the corners and the other players (whites) start by sitting down and defending their cone gate.

The practice begins as the red players run with the ball at speed towards the white players, and as they get close to them, perform one change of direction to dribble past them.

The first red player to enter the central square scores a point. If the defender wins the ball, the players change roles.

Progressions

1. The defenders stand up instead of sitting (as shown in the diagram).
2. The dribbling player can use two changes of direction to beat their opponent and dribble through the cone gate.

Chapter 1: Running with the Ball at Speed

RWTB at Speed to Lose a Marker (Shadowing in Pairs)

8-10 min

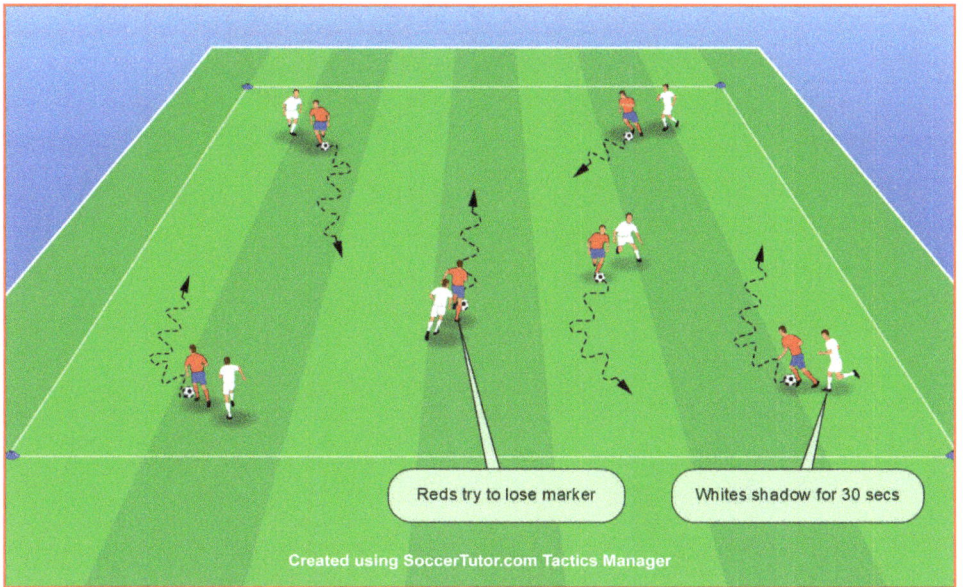

Reds try to lose marker | Whites shadow for 30 secs

Objective: Running with the ball at speed and with good control to lose a marker and retain possession of the ball.

Description

In a 15 x 15 yard area, the players are in pairs. One player has a ball and tries to keep it away from the defender who shadows him.

The ball carrier must try to run with the ball at maximum speed to try and get out of the shadow. The shadow (defender) must follow the movements of the player with the ball for 30 seconds, after which they exchange roles.

If a player manages to keep possession of the ball and stay within the area for 30 seconds, they score a point.

Progression

We start with the defender being passive - you can progress all the way up to a fully active defender, depending on the level of the players.

Chapter 1: Running with the Ball at Speed

RWTB at Speed "Collect the Treasure Game"

10 min

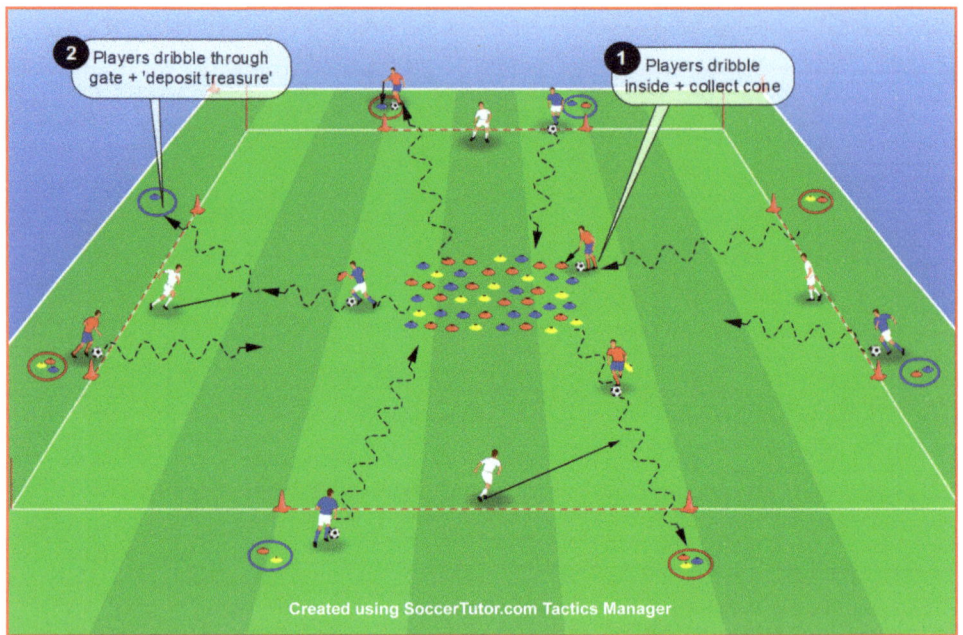

Description

In a 25 x 25 yard area, we mark out a 20 x 20 yard square with 4 cone gates and lots of cones (treasure) in the centre. We have 4 white players guarding the gates, as shown.

In the outside square, there are 2 hoops behind each gate and we start with 4 blue players and 4 red players, each with a ball.

1. They start by dribbling inside to pick up a cone.
2. They then must try to dribble past one of the white defenders and through a cone gate to put the 'treasure' inside their team's hoop.

The players repeat this for the entirety of the practice, trying to get as much treasure as they can. The team with the most treasure collected within a set time wins the game. If a white defender touches or wins the ball, that player who lost it must then try to enter/exit through another cone gate.

Progressions

1. Force the players to change gates each time they collect a cone - they cannot go back to the same place.
2. The players have to use a change of direction to beat the defender through the cone gate.

CHAPTER 2

Dribbling Past Opponents & 1 v 1 Duels

DRIBBLING PAST OPPONENTS TRAINING METHODOLOGY

- It is necessary to work a lot on dribbling past opponents throughout the season, as it is a very useful skill in all competitive games.

- It must be instilled that dribbling is very useful but should be done when it is necessary - the closer you are to the opposition's goal, the better.

- The aim is for players to develop dribbling techniques with changes of direction to beat opponents on both sides (right and left).

- Young players tend to dribble always to one side, so through training they can learn to perform equally well on both sides.

- The players must learn to run with the ball at speed and learn the timing of when to shift the ball away from their opponent.

- As the next step in development, the players can learn specific moves to beat defenders, which can be constantly repeated throughout the practices and speeded up as their technical level increases.

Chapter 2: Dribbling Past Opponents & 1 v 1 Duels

Moves to Beat Defenders in a Continuous Cycle

8-10 min

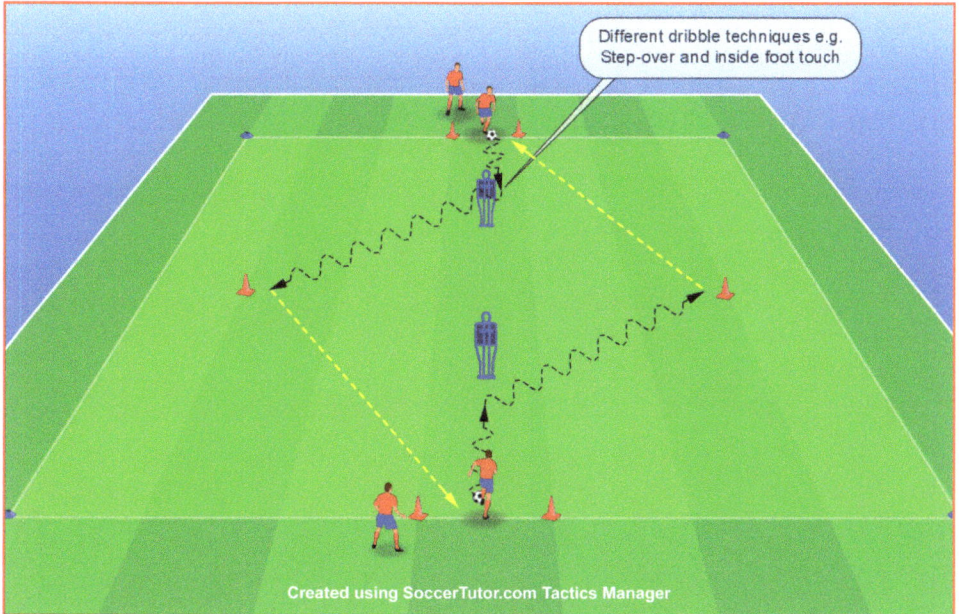

Description

We mark out a 15 yard square and position the cones and mannequins (or large cones) in the positions shown. We have 4 players and the practice starts with 2 balls simultaneously from opposite ends.

The players run forward with the ball and then dribble past the mannequin (using a move to beat a defender) towards the cone on the right side. When they reach the cone, they pass to the opposite end and follow their pass. It is a continuous cycle.

Every two minutes we change the move - here are some examples:

a. "Scissor" (step-over) and touch away with the inside of the same foot.
b. "Scissor" (step-over) and touch away with the outside of the opposite foot.
c. "The chop" - Run forward with the ball, put your leading foot forward and then use the inside of the back foot to push the ball away from the defender.
d. "Double Scissor" (step-over) and touch away with the inside or outside of the foot.

Progressions

1. Perform a second move to beat a defender before making the pass.
2. Replace the mannequin (or large cone) with a passive defender that the players must beat.

Chapter 2: Dribbling Past Opponents & 1 v 1 Duels

Dribbling to Beat an Opponent in a Zonal 1 v 1 Duel

8-10 min

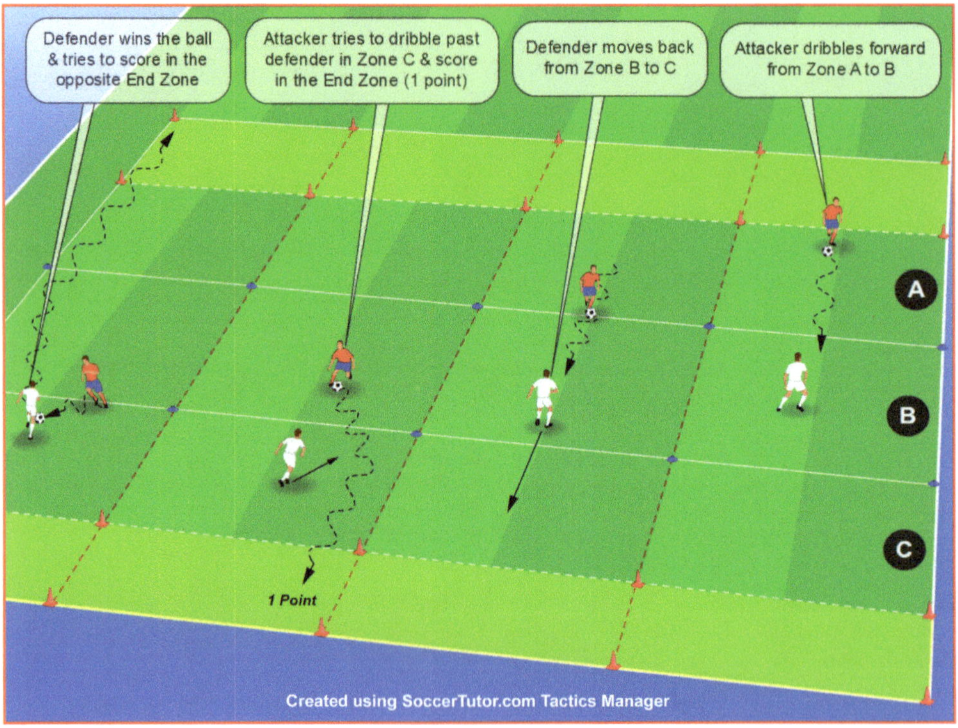

Description

For this practice, we have 1 v 1 channels with 3 zones that are 5 yards long (A-C) + 2 yellow end zones (2.5 yards). The aim is to dribble past the defender and into the end zone to score a point. However, there are specific steps to take:

1. The attacker (red) starts running forward with the ball in Zone A and into Zone B.
2. The defender (white) moves back from Zone B to Zone C. There he will prepare for the attacker, modifying his body position and choosing the right moment to contest the attacker and try to recover the ball.
3. The attacker tries to dribble past the defender in Zone C and into the end zone (1 point).
4. If the defender (white) wins the ball, he tries to run with the ball to the opposite end zone (1 point) and the red player tries to recover the ball. Whatever happens, we start again with the red player.

Halfway through the practice, change the roles of the players.

Chapter 2: Dribbling Past Opponents & 1 v 1 Duels

Dribbling to Beat an Opponent in an End to End Practice

8-10 min

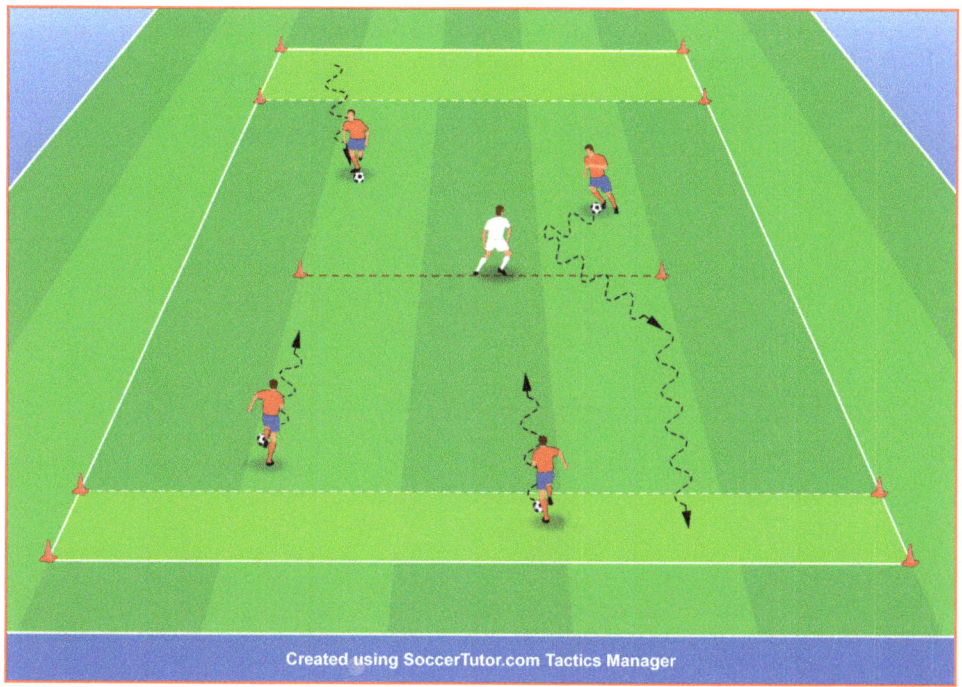

Objective: Dribbling against front-on defender with changes of direction and different techniques.

Description

In a 10 x 20 yard area, we mark two end zones and a cone gate in the centre which is defended by 1 player. On each side, there are 2 or more players with a ball.

The aim is to run with the ball from one end zone to the other by using a move to beat a defender and dribble through the central cone gate.

The players continue to go from one end to the other through the cone gate. If the defender wins the ball or kicks the ball out of the area, he switches roles with the player who lost the ball.

Progressions

1. Reduce the size of the cone gate to increase the difficulty.
2. Add a second defender trying to win the ball.
3. Perform all the dribbling moves with the weaker foot.

Chapter 2: Dribbling Past Opponents & 1 v 1 Duels

Dribbling Past Opponents "Bulldog Game"

8 min

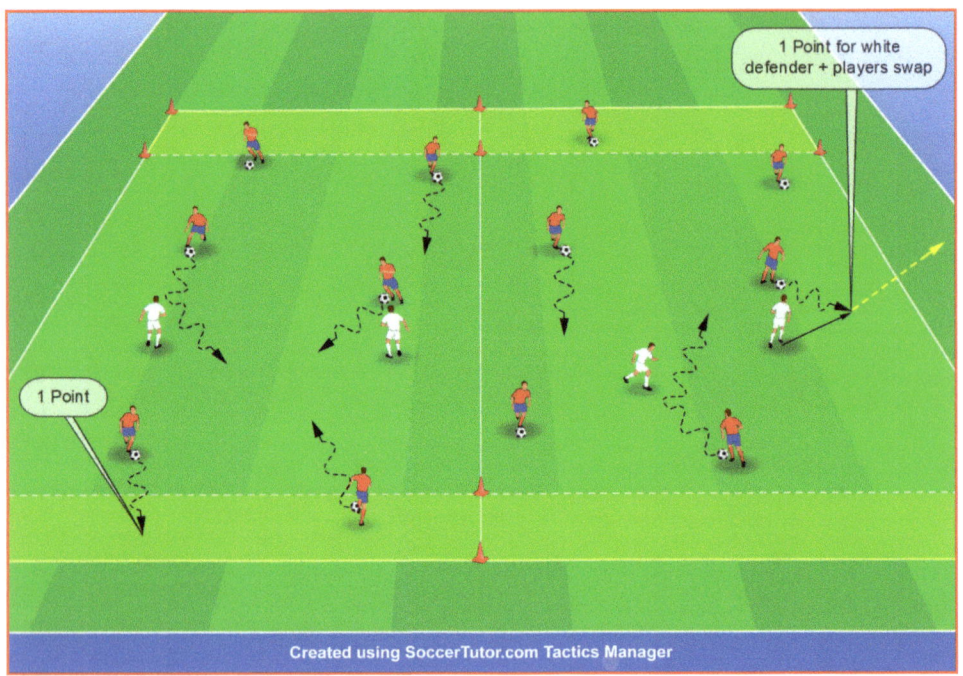

Objective: Dribbling against front-on defenders with changes of direction and different techniques in a continuous game.

Description

For this "Bulldog Game", we split the players into groups of 6-8. Each group plays in a 10 x 30 yard area. Two players act as defenders, as the other players dribble from one end zone to the other - each time they are able to do this they score a point.

If a defender wins the ball or kicks the ball out of the area, they score 2 points and switch roles with the player who lost the ball.

The player with the most points at the end wins.

Progressions

1. Perform the practice with teams and equal numbers e.g. 3 v 3 - three attackers have 4 minutes to see how many points they can score against 3 defenders. Switch roles for the next 4 minutes and see which team scores the most points.
2. Perform all the dribbling moves with the weaker foot.

Chapter 2: Dribbling Past Opponents & 1 v 1 Duels

Dribbling Past Opponents and Keeping the Ball "One Minute Game"

5-7 min

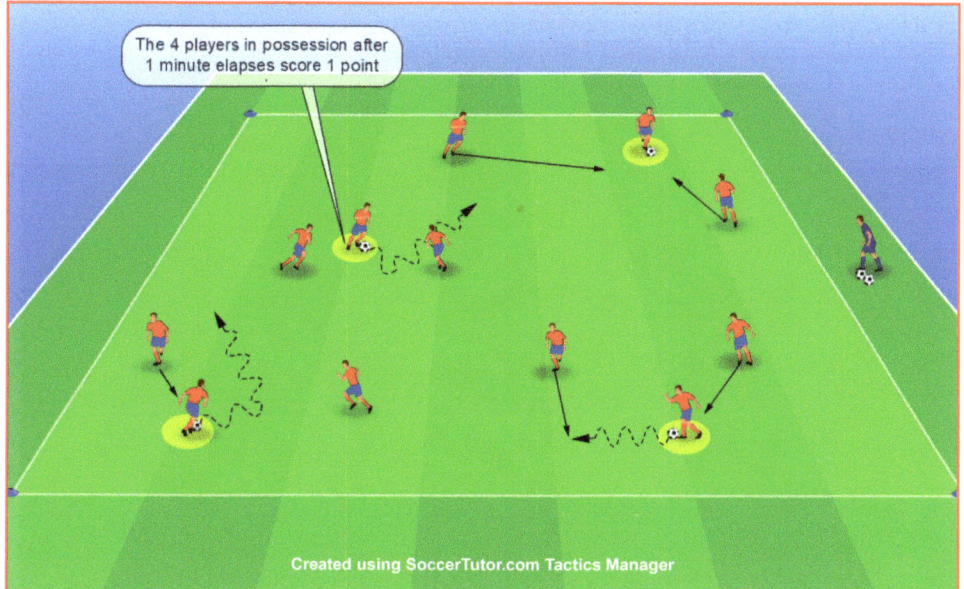

The 4 players in possession after 1 minute elapses score 1 point

Objective: Continuous dribbling past opponents under pressure.

Description

In this "One Minute Game" we play all against all in a 20 x 20 yard area.

In this example we have 12 players and 4 balls - you can change this depending on the age/level of the players. You can simply have 4 players start with a ball or place 4 balls in the middle to start.

Each player with a ball must try to dribble past their opponents and maintain possession of the ball. When the minute is up, the 4 players in possession of the ball all score a point.

We play a few games (5-7) and the first player to score 3 points wins.

Progressions

1. After each "One Minute Game" we remove a ball, so the difficulty of the practice increases a lot.
2. Do not let the players simply keep close technical control of the ball or shield it - they must continuously face their opponents and try to dribble the ball past them.

Chapter 2: Dribbling Past Opponents & 1 v 1 Duels

Dribbling Past Opponents & Through Cone Gates in 1 v 1 Situations

8-10 min

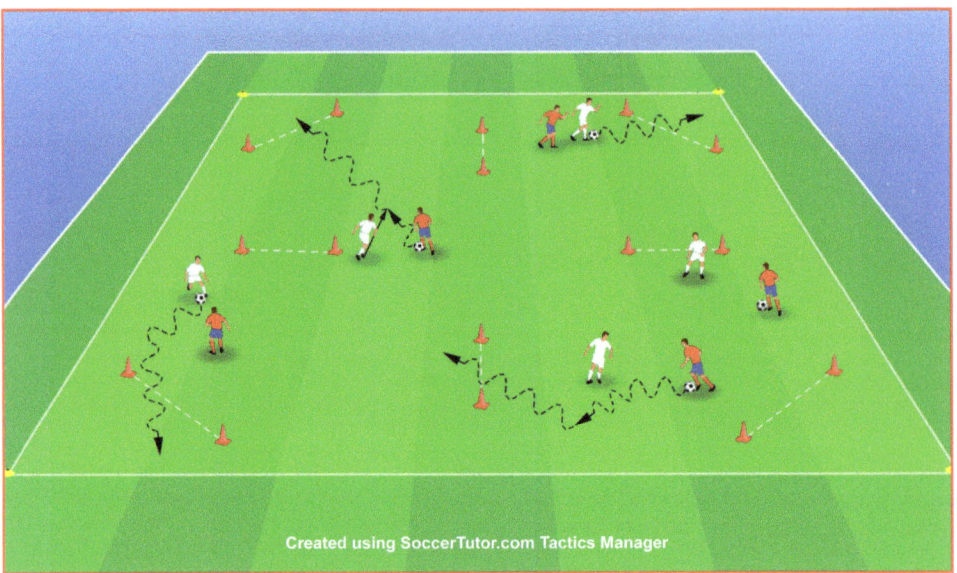

Objective: Accurate dribbling with both feet to beat opponents.

Description

In a 20 yard square, we have 10-12 players and 8 cone gates as shown. The red players each start with a ball and the white players defend the cone gates.

The aim is to approach a defender and dribble past him, then dribble through a cone gate. Each time this happens, they score 1 point for their team.

If a defender wins the ball, they score 1 point and switch roles with the attacking player.

Variations

1. Perform all the dribbling moves with the weaker foot.
2. The players who are defending must do so with their legs together. This makes it easier for the attacking players.

Chapter 2: Dribbling Past Opponents & 1 v 1 Duels

Sprint, Change Direction, Receive, Beat Opponent + Finish

8-10 min

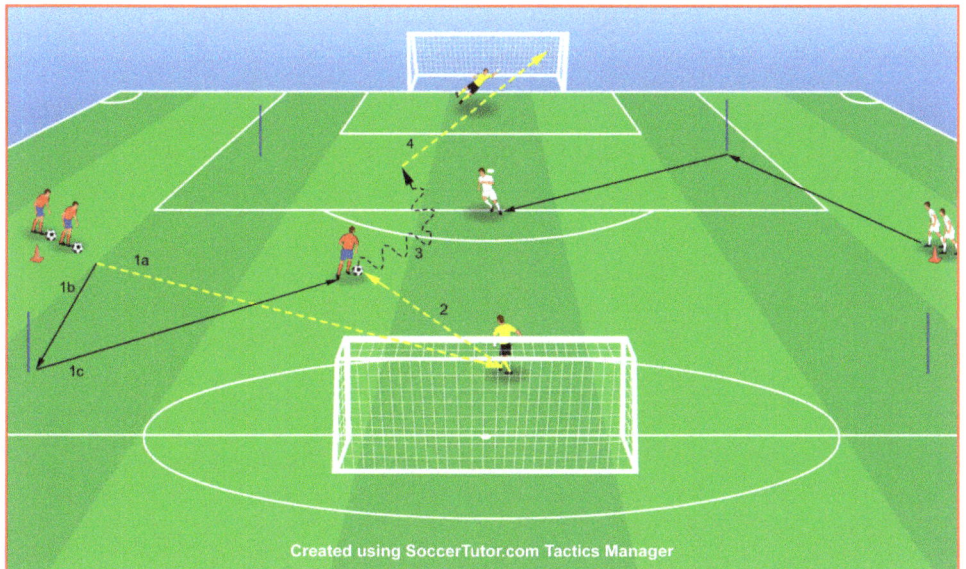

Objective: Receiving and dribbling past opponents quickly to score.

Description

In this practice using half a youth pitch, we have 6 outfield players (2 teams of 3) and 2 goals with goalkeepers. The 2 teams start in parallel positions on either side.

To start the practice, the red player passes to the goalkeeper and sprints to the pole. He then changes direction and runs forward to receive the pass back from the goalkeeper. At the same time, the white player has performed the same run (opposite side and end) and is ready to defend the goal.

The red player must dribble past the defender and try to score. If he does this, he scores a point for his team - if the defender wins the ball or kicks it out of play, he scores 1 point.

The 2 teams alternate between attacking and defending - the next repetition will start with the white player's pass to the goalkeeper and him being the attacker.

Progressions

1. The goal is worth double if the attacker scores directly within 7 seconds of receiving the pass and without the defender touching the ball.
2. Play 2 v 2 - the emphasis is still on dribbling past a defender to score (not passing).

©SoccerTutor.com   *Spanish Football Federation Coaching*

Quick Reactions and Dribbling Past Opponents in 1 v 1 Duels

10-15 min

Objective: Quick reactions and dribbling past opponents in 1 v 1 situations.

Description

In a 30 x 30 yard area, we have two teams positioned in opposite corners and numbered 1-6. There are also 2 goals with goalkeepers and the coach is outside with plenty of balls.

Each player is assigned a number and the coach calls out these numbers as often as he likes. When a number is called, those two players run to the middle to compete for the ball thrown in by the coach.

We then have a 1 v 1 situation and the attacker must try to dribble past their opponent to score. If the defender wins the ball, he tries to then score at the opposite end. If the ball goes out of play, the players return to their start positions.

Variation

The coach can call out 2 or 3 numbers and only throw one ball, making the players compete in 2 v 2 or 3 v 3 duels. However, the focus is still for the ball carrier to dribble past an opponent and shoot (not passing).

CHAPTER 3

Duels (2v1, 2v2, 3v1, 3v2, 3v3)

Chapter 3: Duels (2v1, 2v2, 3v1, 3v2, 3v3)

DUELS TRAINING METHODOLOGY

- The previous two chapters 'Running with the Ball at Speed' and 'Dribbling Past Opponents' provide the foundation for training duels.

- Duels are fundamental for the development and knowledge of this game. We carry out mini-matches in small spaces, with different aims and variations to train players for duels that they will face throughout their careers.

- How many times in a football match is there a 1 v 1 duel? Or a 2 v 1? Or a 2 v 2? Honestly, a lot, at all times! We practice these up to 3 v 3 which occur in games often. The more you train for these duels, the more ideas the players will have when these situations occur in competitive matches.

Chapter 3: Duels (2v1, 2v2, 3v1, 3v2, 3v3)

Lose Marker, Receive and Pass Back

8-10 min

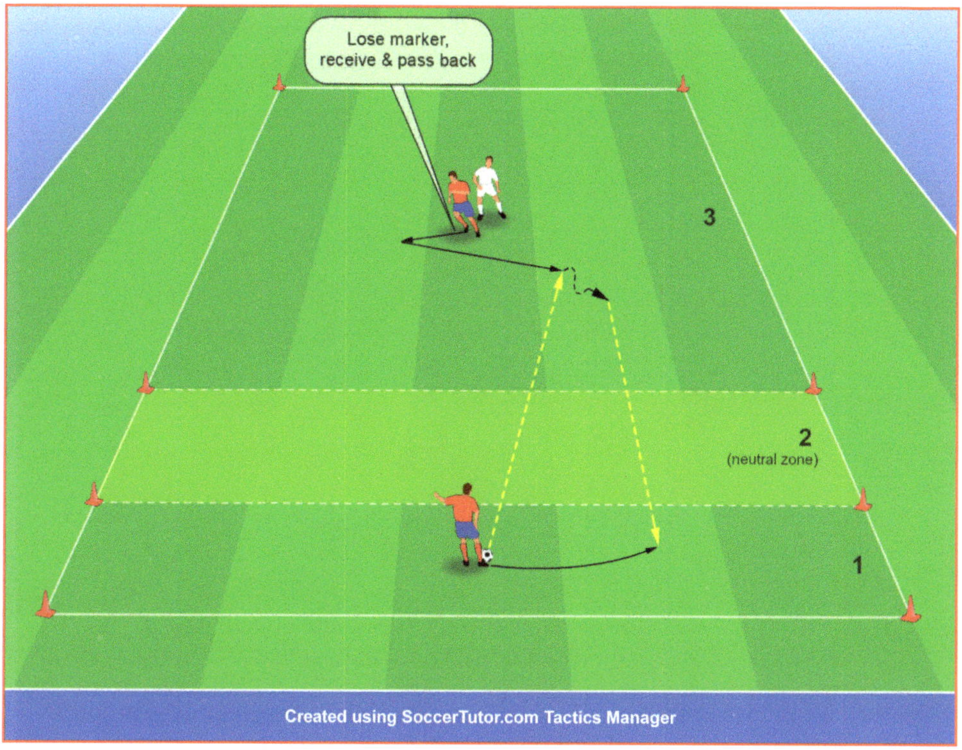

Objective: Checking away from a marker to receive in space (1 v 1).

Description

In a 10 x 20 yard area, we mark out 3 zones as shown. In the first zone, we have a player with a ball. The second zone is an empty 'neutral zone' where no player can enter at any time. In the third and largest zone, we have 1 attacker and 1 defender.

The aim for the attacker is to check away from the defender and move to receive the pass in space. If the attacker is able to lose his marker, he should be able to receive and play back to his teammate in the first zone (1 point).

The defender tries to intercept the pass and win the ball (1 point).

After a set time, change the roles of the players.

Variations

1. Change the roles of the players each time the defender is able to win the ball.
2. The player is limited to 1 touch - first time pass back.

Chapter 3: Duels (2v1, 2v2, 3v1, 3v2, 3v3)

Quick Attack in a 2 v 1 (+1 Supporting Player) Duel

8-10 min

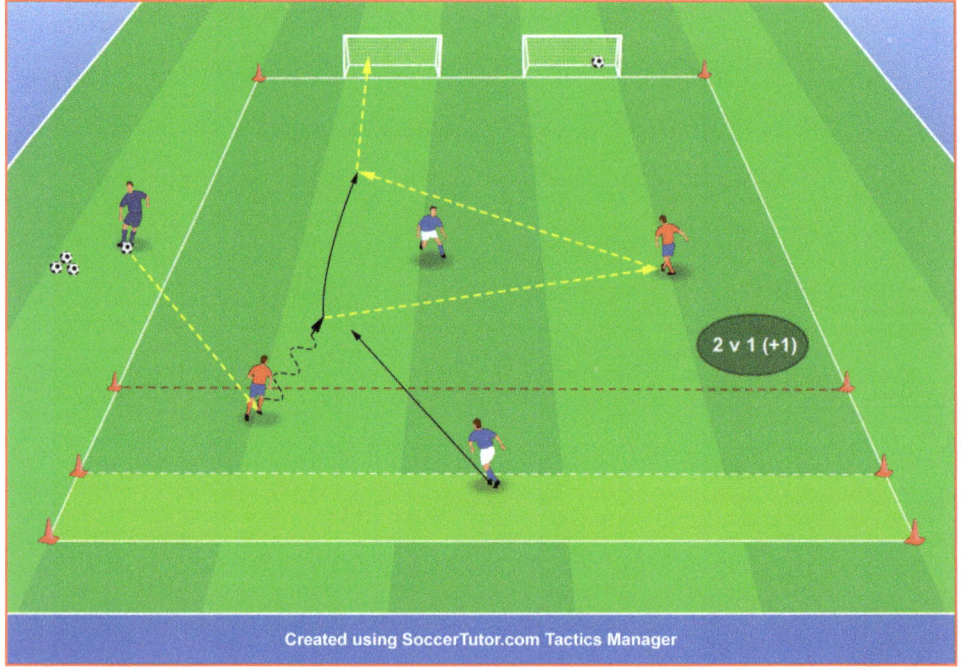

Objective: Taking advantage of a 2 v 1 situation quickly, before defensive support arrives.

Description

In a 15 x 20 yard area, we mark out a 5 yard zone at one end as shown.

The coach starts the practice by passing the ball to the deepest red player and we initially have a 2 v 1 situation, with the reds trying to score quickly in either of the 2 small goals. There is an extra blue player who starts in the end zone - he can move back to defend as soon as a red player touches the ball.

The first blue player aims to hold up (delay) the reds attack, giving time for the second blue player to run back and help defend, thus creating a numerical equality.

The red team will have 5 attacks and then the teams change roles. The team that scores the most goals wins.

Variation

If the defending team manage to win the ball, they then aim to dribble the ball into the end zone or receive a pass inside it to score a goal.

Chapter 3: Duels (2v1, 2v2, 3v1, 3v2, 3v3)

Dribbling and Shooting with 2 v 1 Duel

10 min

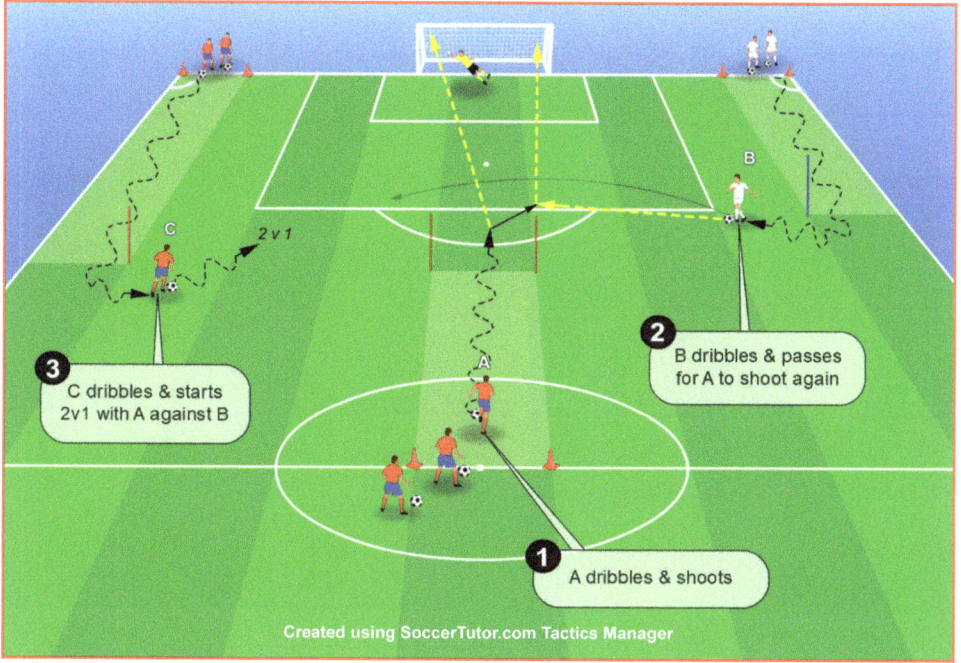

Objective: To practice dribbling at speed, shooting and 2 v 1 duels.

Description

Using half a youth pitch, we have 3 stations as shown.

On the coach's whistle, 3 players (A, B & C) start running with the ball at the same time:

1. Player A dribbles forward quickly, through the poles and shoots from the edge of the penalty area.

2. Player B dribbles around the pole and passes for A to shoot again.

3. Player C initially dribbles slower than the other players, then joins to create a 2 v 1 duel. A and C are the attackers versus B, who acts as the defender.

Player B must be focussed and react quickly to defend in the 2 v 1 duel. Change the roles of the players each time the reds fail to score.

Chapter 3: Duels (2v1, 2v2, 3v1, 3v2, 3v3)

One-Two, Receive and 2 v 1 Duel

8-10 min

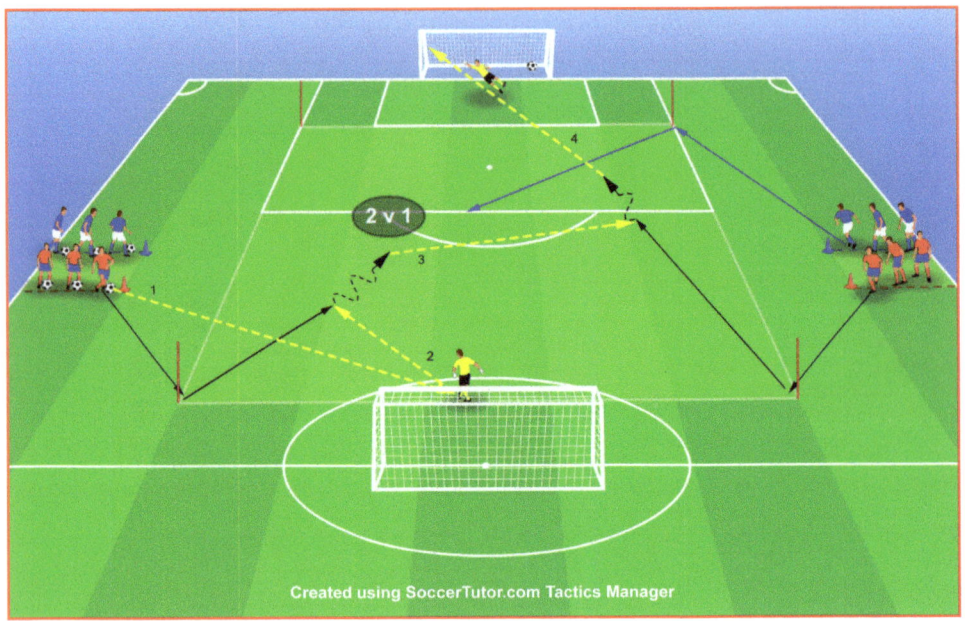

Objective: Fast 2 v 1 play in the final third.

Description

Using half a youth pitch, we have 2 teams with 6 players each. They start alternately with a ball. We also have 2 large goals with goalkeepers.

In the diagram, the red player starts with a pass to the goalkeeper, sprints back to the pole and then forward as shown. At the same time, a teammate on the opposite side makes parallel movements - as does a blue player at the other end.

The goalkeeper returns a pass to the red player who receives and starts a 2 v 1 attack. From this point, the 2 attackers should try to score within 7 seconds (1 point).

The blue player defends the goal and tries to win the ball (1 point).

Progression

Change the situation to 2 v 2 with 1 player from each team taking part on both sides.

Chapter 3: Duels (2v1, 2v2, 3v1, 3v2, 3v3)

2 v 2 (+1) Duel Game with 4 Goals

10 min

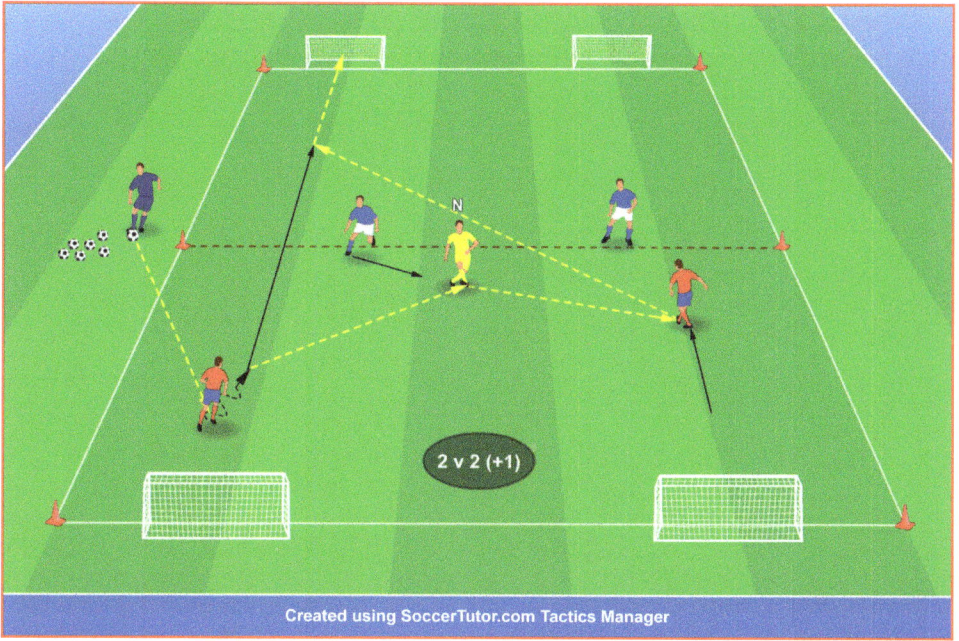

Objective: To practice fast 3 v 2 (2 v 2 +1) duels.

Description

Within a 10 x 15 yard area, we have 2 teams with 2 players + 1 yellow neutral player. There are 2 small goals at each end.

The practice starts with the coach who passes to one of the players. In the diagram example, the red players attack with the neutral player (3 v 2) and try to score in the 2 small goals at the far end.

The blue players defend and try to win the ball. When an attack is finished, the ball goes out of play or the blues win the ball, the coach passes a new ball to a blue player and they launch a 3 v 2 attack with the neutral player towards the opposite end.

Variations

1. Add a halfway line (red dashed line in the diagram). In order for the goal to be valid, all 3 players must be in the attacking half before a goal can be scored.
2. Both teams can score in any of the 4 goals.

Chapter 3: Duels (2v1, 2v2, 3v1, 3v2, 3v3)

Consecutive 2 v 1 Duels with Attackers Split into 2 Side Channels

10 min

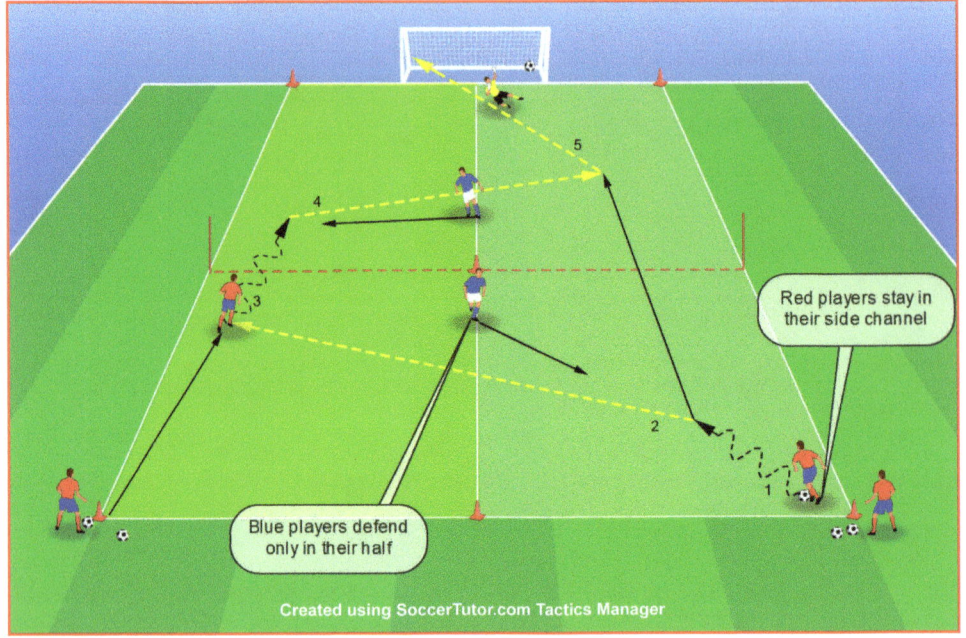

Objective: To practice fast attacks in 2 v 1 situations.

Description

In a 15 x 20 yard area, we split the pitch in half horizontally with 1 blue defender in each half. We also split the pitch in half vertically with 1 red attacker operating on each side.

A red player starts with the ball (right channel). The 2 red players attack with a 2 v 1 situation in the first half, but each player must stay within their side channel.

The first aim is to dribble into the attacking half or receive a pass within it. The next aim is to again attack in a 2 v 1 situation against the other defender and then score past the goalkeeper.

If the attacking pair do not score, they switch roles with the defenders.

Variation

Each pair can defend for a set amount of time and they score a point every time they prevent a goal from being scored.

Chapter 3: Duels (2v1, 2v2, 3v1, 3v2, 3v3)

Awareness, Quick Reactions to Receive and 2 v 2 Duels

10 min

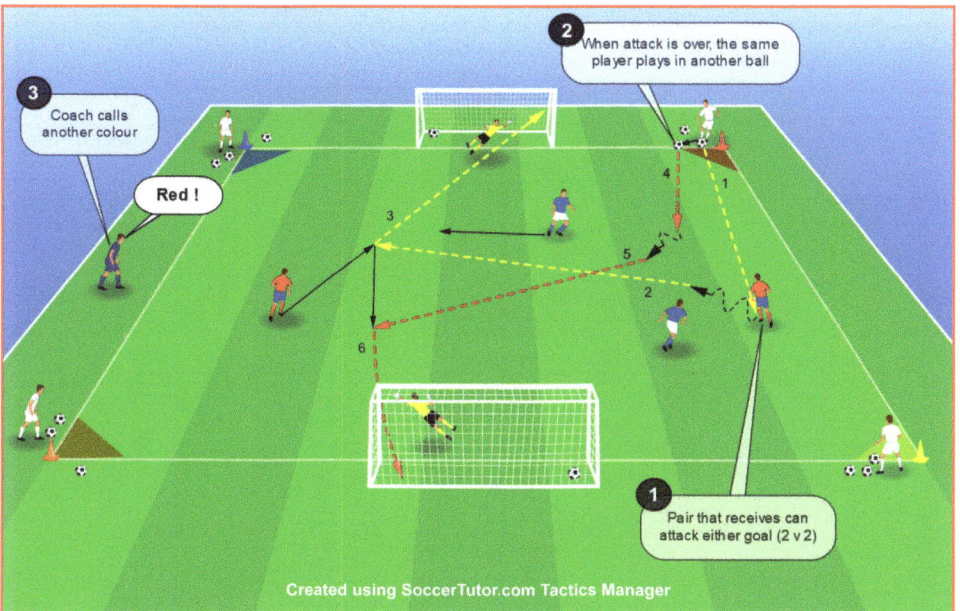

Objective: To develop awareness, quick reactions and 2 v 2 play.

Description

In a 20 x 20 yard area, we have 2 v 2 inside + 2 goals with goalkeepers. There are also 4 feeder players in the corners, each next to a cone of a different colour.

The practice starts when the coach calls out a colour. The attacking pair (reds in diagram) must receive from the player next to the cone of the same colour and then try to score.

When the attack is over, they again receive a ball from the same player. After the second ball, the coach calls out a new colour.

The attacking pair receive 2 balls from each corner and a total of 8 balls. They see how many goals they can score, before the teams switch roles. The blue players then see how many goals they can score with their 8 balls.

Variations

1. Change the practice so that the attacking players call out the colour each time a new ball is needed.
2. Headed goals count double.

Chapter 3: Duels (2v1, 2v2, 3v1, 3v2, 3v3)

Fast Attack in a 3 v 2 Duel

2 x 5 min

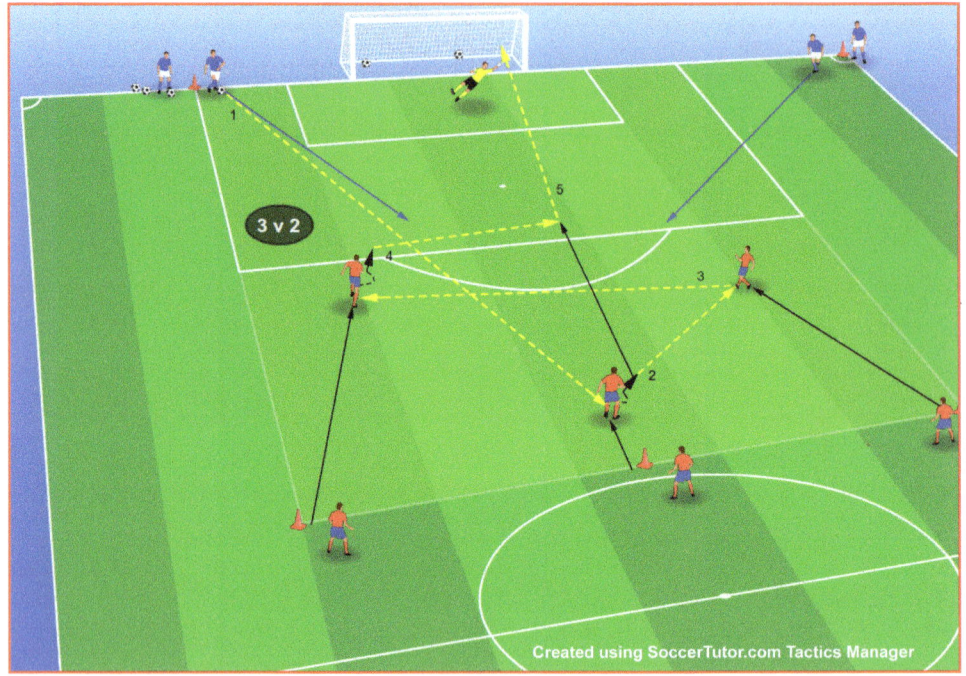

Objective: Quick combination play and attacking in a 3 v 2 duel.

Description

Within half a youth pitch, we position 5 cones to act as starting points in the positions shown. There are 2 players starting on each cone.

We start with a blue player from the by-line who passes to the central red player. The other 2 red players move forward off their cone and the 2 blue players move forward to defend the 3 v 2 situation as soon as the pass is received.

The red players must try to finish their attack in the shortest possible time. The blue players defend the goal and try to win the ball.

After an attack is finished, repeat with the next players who are waiting. After a set time, change the roles of the players (attackers become defenders and vice versa).

Variation

Start the practice with a pass from an attacking player.

©SoccerTutor.com — Spanish Football Federation Coaching

Chapter 3: Duels (2v1, 2v2, 3v1, 3v2, 3v3)

1 v 1 Duels into Collective 3 v 2 Duel

12 min

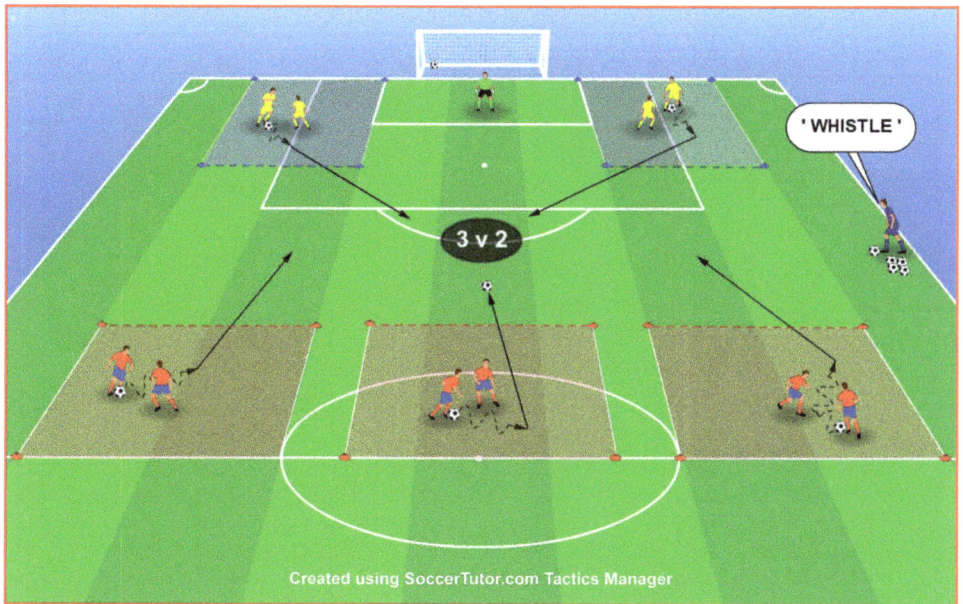

Objective: To develop competitive 1 v 1 duels and a game specific 3 v 2 duel.

Description

Using half a youth pitch, we mark out 3 red squares and 2 blue squares as shown. We also have a large goal with a goalkeeper.

Within each square we have a 1 v 1 duel. The pairs compete in consecutive 1 v 1 duels within the areas until the coach blows his whistle.

The 3 red players in possession then leave their squares and move forward to launch an attack and try to score. The central player is the one to collect the ball in the middle and start the 3 v 2 attack.

The 2 yellow players in possession also leave their square and are ready to defend the goal for the 3 v 2 duel.

Variation

Depending on the number of players, include an additional square to have a 4 v 2 duel or remove a defensive square for a 3 v 1.

Chapter 3: Duels (2v1, 2v2, 3v1, 3v2, 3v3)

Continuous 2 (+2) v 2 Duels with Two Goals

8-10 min

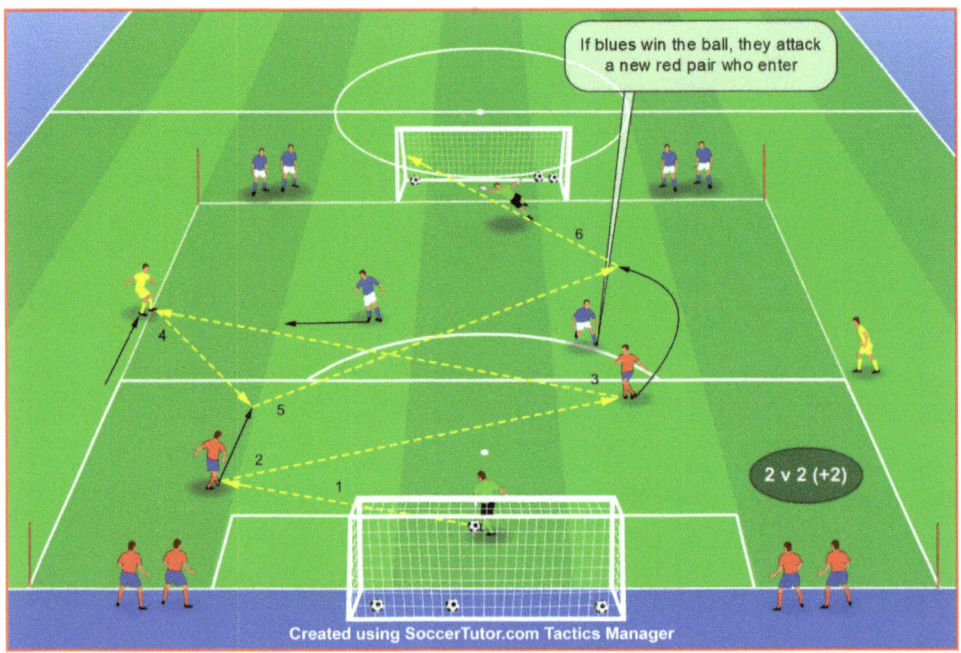

Objective: Fast attacks in 2 v 2 duels using support players.

Description

Using an area double the size of a youth penalty box, we have 2 teams competing, each with 3 pairs. We also have 2 yellow neutral players (1 on each side) + 2 goals with goalkeepers.

The practice starts with a goalkeeper. The 2 attacking players (reds in diagram) try to score quickly, making sure to use their numerical advantage with the 2 neutral yellow side players.

If the blues win the ball, they attack the goal at the opposite end and try to score. They attack a new red pair who enter - the old pair leave the area.

If a goal is scored, the goalkeeper saves or the ball goes out of play, the goalkeeper at that end restarts the game with the next 2 pairs who enter the area.

Variation

Remove the yellow neutral side players and make it a simple and fast 2 v 2.

Chapter 3: Duels (2v1, 2v2, 3v1, 3v2, 3v3)

Continuous 3 v 3 Duel Team Game

15 min

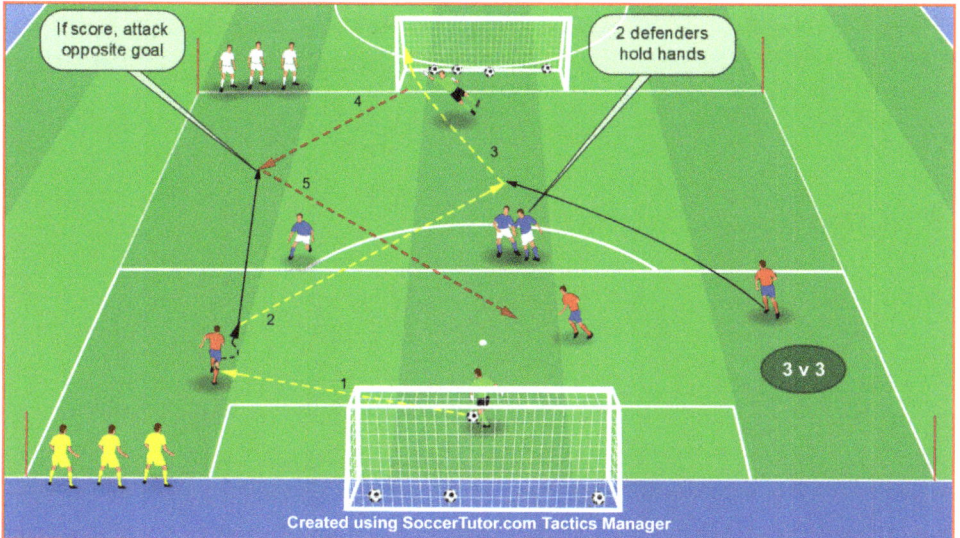

Description

Using an area double the size of a youth penalty box, we have 4 teams competing, each with 3 players.

The practice starts with the goalkeeper and the 3 attacking players (reds in diagram) trying to score as quickly as possible. There are 3 blue players, 2 of which must hold hands while defending.

If the red attacking team score, they continue and receive from the goalkeeper at that end to start a new attack towards the opposite end (see red arrows in diagram). The blue defending team leave the pitch to be replaced by a new team (it would be the yellows in the diagram example).

If the blue team win the ball, they become the attackers and the reds leave the pitch. The goalkeeper passes a new ball in for the blues and a new team (yellows) have to defend.

If the goalkeeper saves or the ball goes out of play, the goalkeeper at that end restarts the game - both teams leave the pitch and the next 2 teams enter.

Variations

1. The defenders do not need to hold hands if it goes well and there are plenty of goals scored.
2. Players can only score with their weaker foot.

CHAPTER 4

Passing

Chapter 4: Passing

PASSING TRAINING METHODOLOGY

- Passing is one of the main foundations in our football school, one of the most repeated words for all of our coaches "Pass, pass, pass ...".

- We practice passes that reflect passes that players will use during competitive games.

- As well as focussing on the technical aspects of different passes (short, medium, long), we also work on receiving on the move.

- We use a mixture of practices where players pass and move in fixed positions and others where they pass more freely in pairs.

- Depending on the ages we work with, we will adjust the passing distances for the practices.

- For the younger players, it is very important that they gain confidence. Therefore, we will perform many of the practices with hardly any opposition or with some passive resistance as a progression.

Chapter 4: Passing

Dribble + One-Two in a Passing Square

10 min

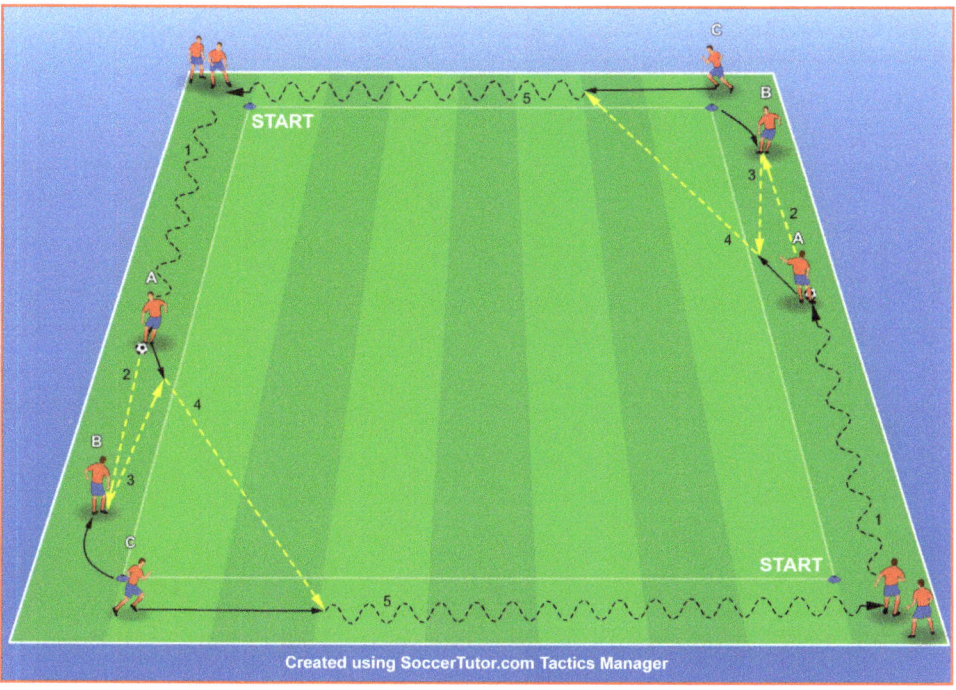

Objective: To practice short passing (with one-twos) on the move.

Description

Mark out a square to suit the age/level of the players. We have a total of 10-12 players - there are 4 players in opposite corners (2 in each - B & C) without a ball and the rest of the players begin in the start positions (A).

The practice starts simultaneously from the 2 start positions. Player A dribbles forward and plays a one-two combination with B who moves off the cone. Player A then passes for C to run onto, who dribbles to the start position and gives the ball to the next player waiting.

The coach keeps changing the direction of play (clockwise/anti-clockwise). The practice can be performed with 2, 3 or 4 balls, but it is recommended to start with 2.

Variation: Instead of dribbling all the way to the next player in the start position, pass to him.

Progression: To increase the difficulty of the practice, limit the players to 1 touch and/or use 3/4 balls at a time.

Spanish Football Federation Coaching

 Chapter 4: Passing

Free Passing in Pairs Against Restricted Defenders

8-10 min

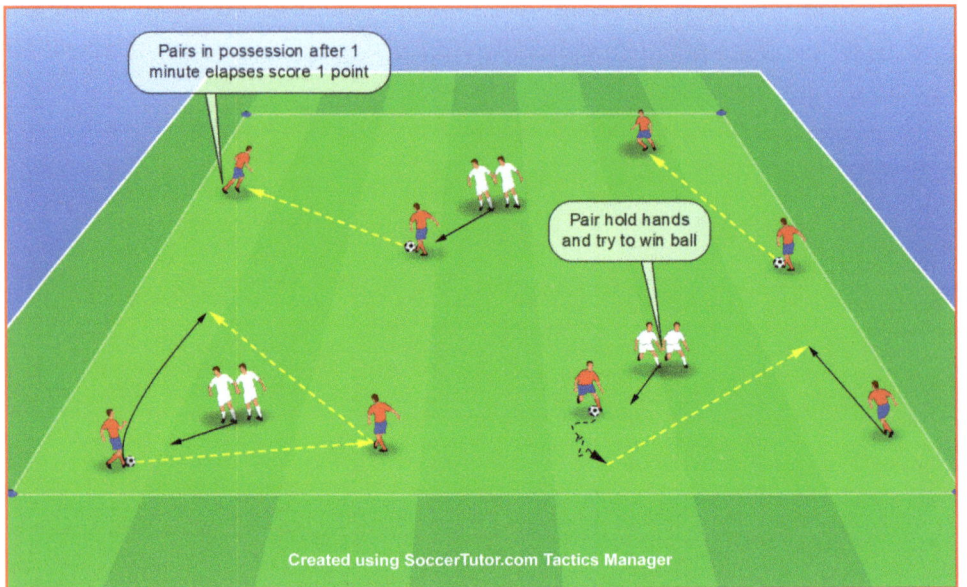

Objective: Passing and receiving in pairs, to beat opponents.

Description

Mark out a 20-30 yard square. In this example we have 7 pairs (total of 14 players).

The red attacking pairs (each with a ball) pass to each other and try to keep possession. The white defending pairs hold hands and try to win the ball.

If a defending pair win the ball, they switch roles with the attacking pair that they won the ball from.

We run the practice for 1 minute. When the minute is over, the pairs that have possession of a ball win a point.

We repeat this one-minute game and the first pair to 3 points wins.

Progressions

1. Limit the players to 2/3 touches.
2. The defending pair do not have to hold hands.

 Chapter 4: Passing

Passing in Continuous 2 v 1 Situations

6-8 min

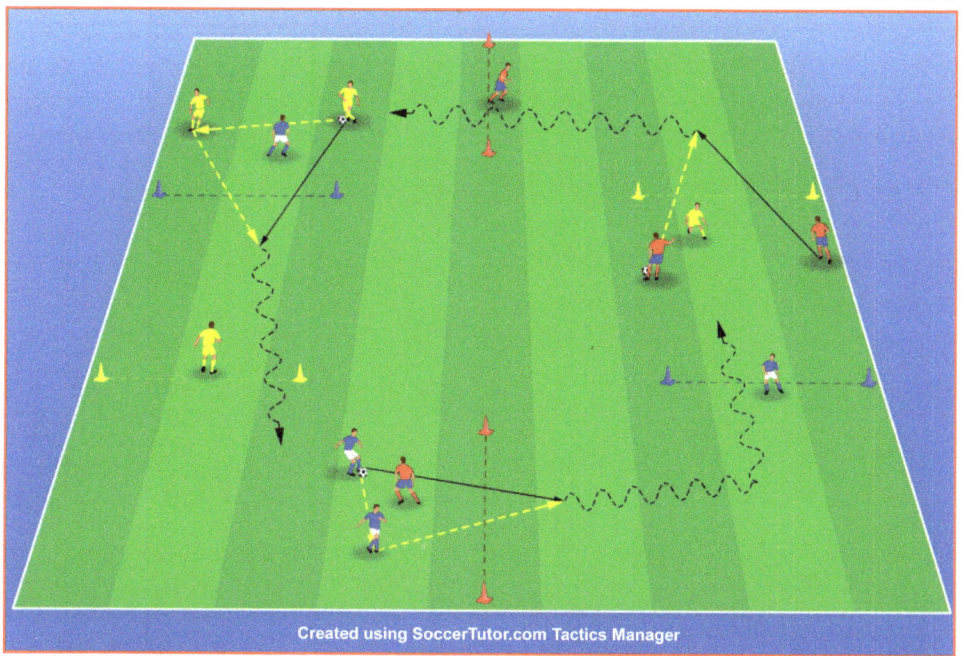

Objective: Passing and receiving in pairs, to beat opponents.

Description

Mark out an area to suit the age/level of the players. We position 6 large cone gates (5 yards) as shown.

We have 3 teams each with 4 players - 2 players defend cone gates and the other pair pass the ball continuously around the circuit.

One player must pass through the cone gate for the other to receive - this can be done with 1 pass or a one-two combination. Each time this is achieved, that team scores 1 point.

If a defender wins the ball or kicks it out of play (1 point), he and the other defender of the same colour become an attacking pair - the pair that were in possession move to defend the cone gates.

Progressions

1. On the coach's whistle, all pairs change direction.
2. Limit the players to a maximum of 1 or 2 touches.

Chapter 4: Passing

One-Two Passing Combinations at Different Angles

4 x 3 min

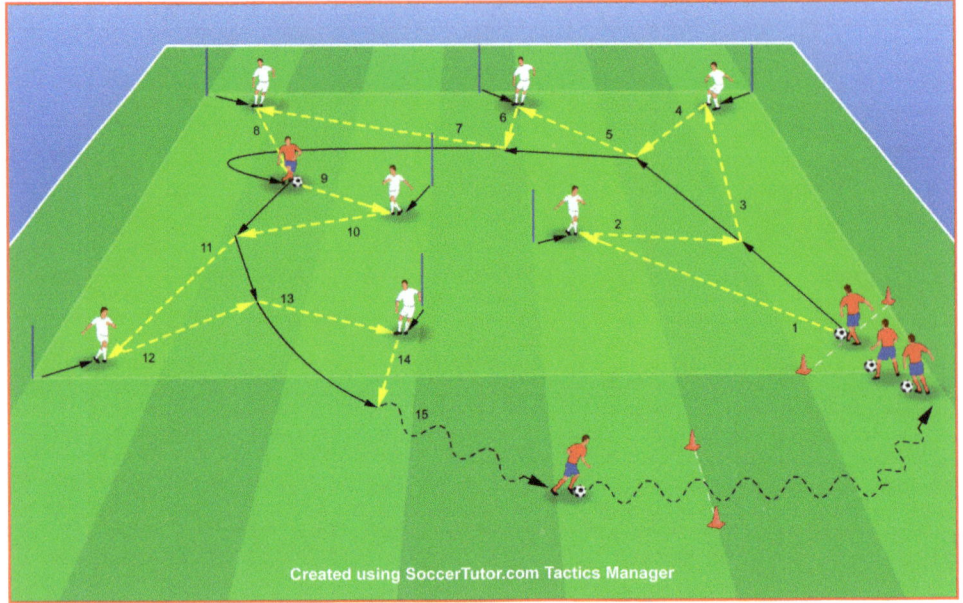

Objective: To develop passing and receiving at different angles with one-two combinations.

Description

Mark out an area to suit the age/level of the players.

We have 7 players (whites) positioned on the cones as shown and the rest of the players (reds) have a ball each.

The red players play one-two combinations with every one of the white players in the sequence shown. When they receive the last pass back, they dribble through the cone gate and back to the start.

Depending on the age/level of the players, start by using 2 touches (control + pass) and then progress to 1 touch passing.

The white players step off their cone to play their passes on the move. We repeat 4 sequences of 3 minutes. Change the roles of the players after each repetition.

Chapter 4: Passing

'Y Shape' Passing Practice with One-Two Combinations

2 x 5 min

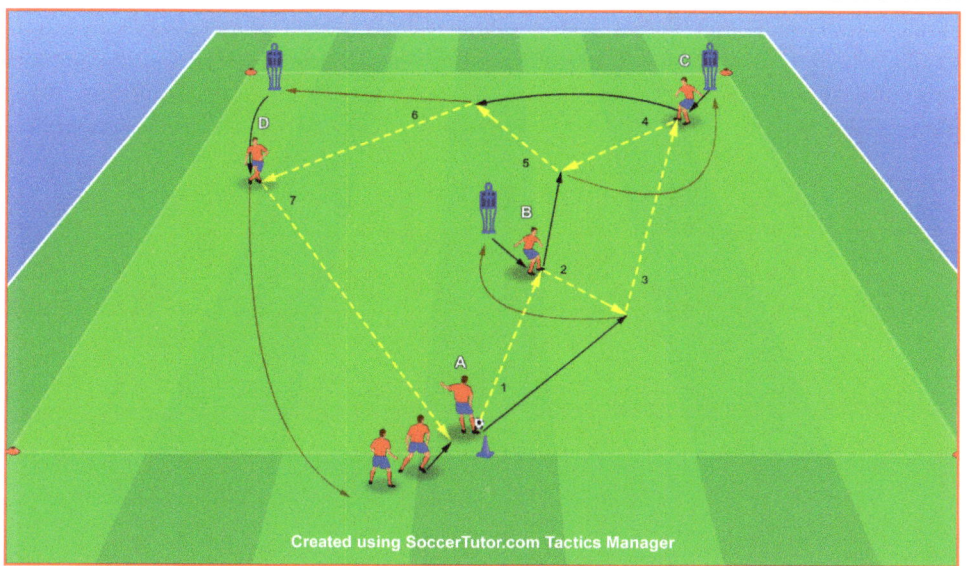

Objective: Quick passing, receiving and movement in tight spaces.

Description

Within a 20 yard square, mark out a 'Y shape' with cones or mannequins, as shown. We have a minimum of 6 players for this practice - 3 players (B, C & D) start next to the mannequins and the rest of the players are at the start position.

There is a specific passing sequence. The players' first movements are shown by the black lines and their movements after their final pass are shown by the red lines.

- The practice starts with A who plays a one-two with B, passes to C and then moves to B's cone.
- B turns to receive the pass from C. Player C moves towards the next cone to receive the next pass from B. Player B moves to C's cone.
- Player D moves off his cone to receive the pass from C and pass to the next player waiting at the start position (C moves to D's cone and D goes to the start).

The passing sequence is continuous with a new player A each time.

Progressions

1. The players must check away from the cone in the opposite direction before moving to receive the next pass.
2. On the coach's whistle, the players change direction (anti-clockwise -> clockwise).

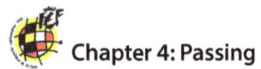

Chapter 4: Passing

Short and Long Passing in a Double Square Practice

8 min

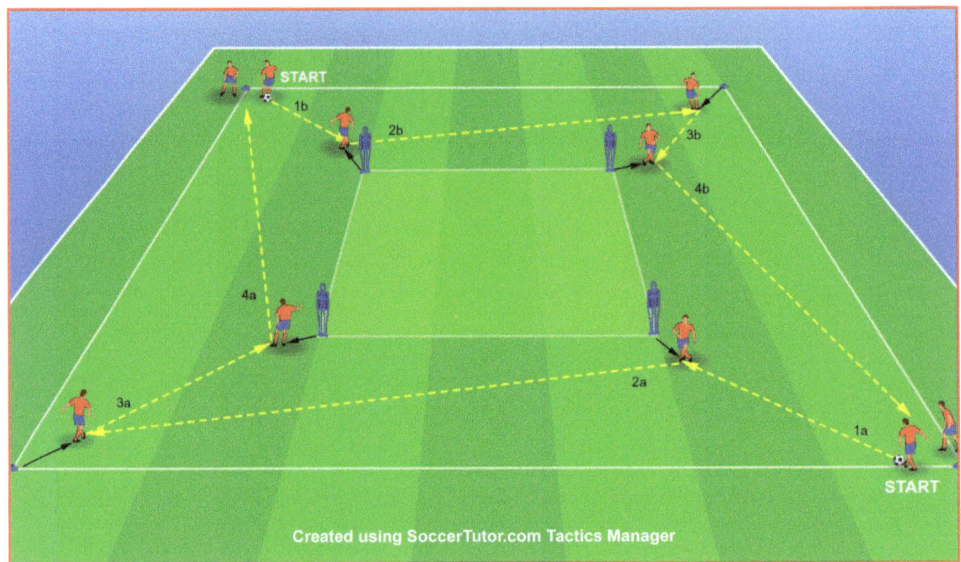

Description

We mark out a 30 yard outer square and a 15 yard inner square. There is one player in each corner of both squares + 1 extra player in each start position as shown.

The practice starts with 2 balls simultaneously in each corner of the outer square. In this example we play in a clockwise direction.

1. The first outside player makes a short pass to the inside player.
2. The inside player moves off the cone and plays a long pass to the next outside player.
3. The outside player moves off the cone and plays a short pass to the next inside player.
4. The inside player passes to the start position - the next player receives and the practice continues.

Each player moves to the next position (follows their pass).

Variations

1. The long passes must be played along the ground, and the next short pass must be with 1 touch.
2. The long pass must be in the air. The next player uses 2 touches - control + pass.
3. You can start with 1 ball and then progress to use 2.

Chapter 4: Passing

Quick One-Two, Pass & Follow in a Double Square Practice

8-10 min

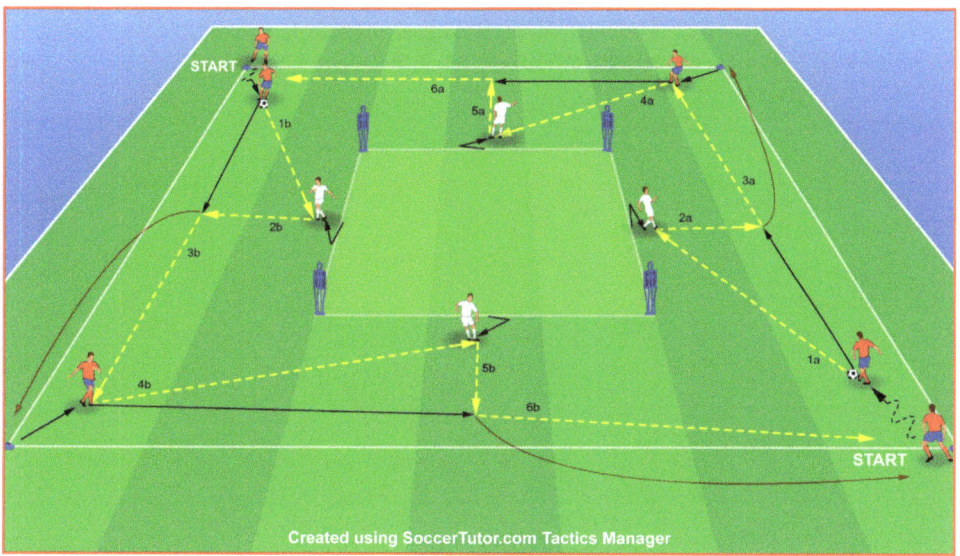

Description

We mark out a 30 yard outer square and a 15 yard inner square. There are 6 red players in the corners of the outside square (2 in each start position). We also have 4 white players in the inside square (1 in the middle of each side as shown).

The practice starts with 2 balls simultaneously in each corner of the outer square. In this example we play in an anti-clockwise direction.

1. The first outside player moves forward with the ball and passes to the inside player.
2. The white inside player passes back (one-two) into the path of the red player.
3. The red player receives back and passes to the next outside red player who moves off the cone.
4. The second outside player passes to the next inside player
5. The white inside player passes back (one-two) into the path of the red player.
6. The red player receives and passes to the start position - the next player receives and the practice continues.

The outside players rotate in an anti-clockwise direction, following their second pass. The inside players stay in their positions so switch the roles of the players often.

Progressions

1. Start by playing with 2 touches and progress to using 1 touch.
2. On the coach's whistle, change the direction of the practice to clockwise.

Chapter 4: Passing

One-Two on the Outside, Pass and Supporting Run on the Inside

10 min

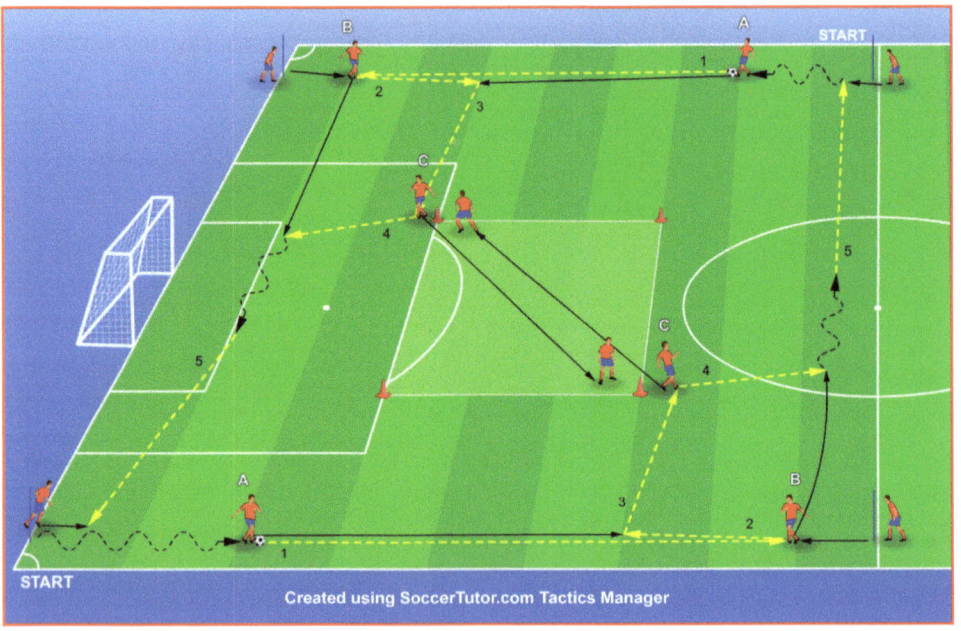

Description

Using half a youth pitch, we have 12-14 players participating with 2 balls. We mark out a central square as shown.

We have a specific passing sequence with 2 balls being used simultaneously from the 2 start positions (in opposite corners).

The practice starts with player A dribbling forward and passing to B. Player B moves off the pole and plays the ball right back (one-two). Player A then passes inside to C, who lays the ball off for B to receive on the run. Player A moves to B's position.

To finish the sequence, B dribbles forward and passes to the next start position.

The inside players (C) stay in their central position but move diagonally to the other side after their pass.

Progressions

1. On the coach's whistle, change the direction of the practice (anti-clockwise -> clockwise).
2. Perform an action (e.g. Jump) before receiving each pass.
3. Play with up to 4 balls.

Chapter 4: Passing

Building Up Play to Pass and Switch Play in a 1 v 1 Channel Game

15 min

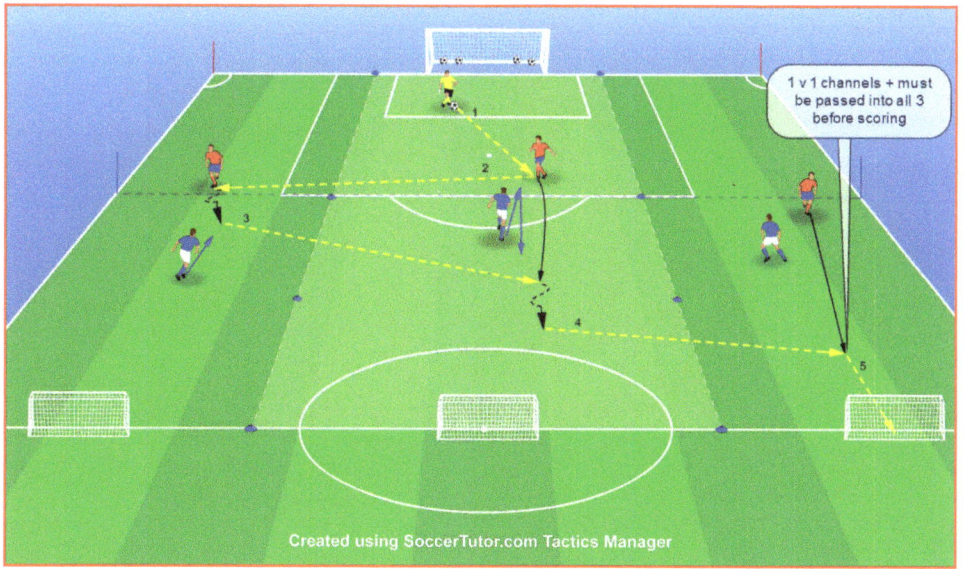

Objective: Building up play from the back with passing and switching play.

Description

Using half a youth pitch, we divide it into 3 equal channels as shown. In each channel, we have a 1 v 1 situation and a small goal at the end.

The red team also have a goalkeeper who starts with the ball in the middle channel. The goalkeeper can pass to red any player within their channel.

The red team build up play and aim to score in one of the small goals - they cannot leave their channel at any point and all 3 players must touch the ball before a goal can be scored. This encourages the team to build up play using good passing and a switch of play.

If a blue player wins the ball, all the blue players can then move freely across the channels to launch a counter attack. The red players become defenders but must still remain within their channel.

Variation

Allow the blue players to move freely across the channels when they're defending.

Chapter 4: Passing

Passing Forward in a 3 Zone Small Sided Game

15 min

Objective: Passing forward (from build up to finish) within a small sided game.

Description

For this 8 v 8 small sided game, we divide the area into 3 equal zones. In the first zone, we have a goalkeeper + 3 red defenders against 1 blue forward. In the middle zone, we have 3 red midfielders against 3 blue midfielders. In the final zone, we have 1 red forward against 3 blue defenders + goalkeeper.

The practice starts from the goalkeeper and the aim is to play through the zones and score. One player can move to the next zone each time - he must run forward to receive a pass, as shown in the diagram. This creates a 4 v 3 situation in the middle zone and a 3 v 2 situation in the final zone.

All of the players on the defending team stay within their zones at all times.

Variation

The players have to complete a certain number of passes within a zone before they are allowed to play forward into the next zone e.g. 4 in first zone, 3 in middle zone.

CHAPTER 5

Rondos

RONDOS TRAINING METHODOLOGY

- Speed, mental agility, technical dexterity and general coordination are some of the skills and physical-technical aspects that are developed by using Rondos in our training sessions.

- Great experts assure that the 5 v 2 Rondo is the most effective. From this starting point you can add the variations that you want to either raise or lower the difficulty (1 touch, 2 touches, weaker foot, keeping the ball up in the air, and more).

- In the RFEF Coaching School, we create many different kinds of Rondos. It is clear that Rondos are a well recommended form of training, but we never leave the player with time and freedom, and instead apply rules and limits. Otherwise the Rondos they perform may be fun but you run the risk of them being monotonous and without specific objectives.

- Coaches should always have specific guidelines and a number of variations depending on the total time spent, which should never be more than 10 minutes per session.

Chapter 5: Rondos

5 v 1 Rondo with 2 Balls (1 with Feet, 1 with Hands)

8 min

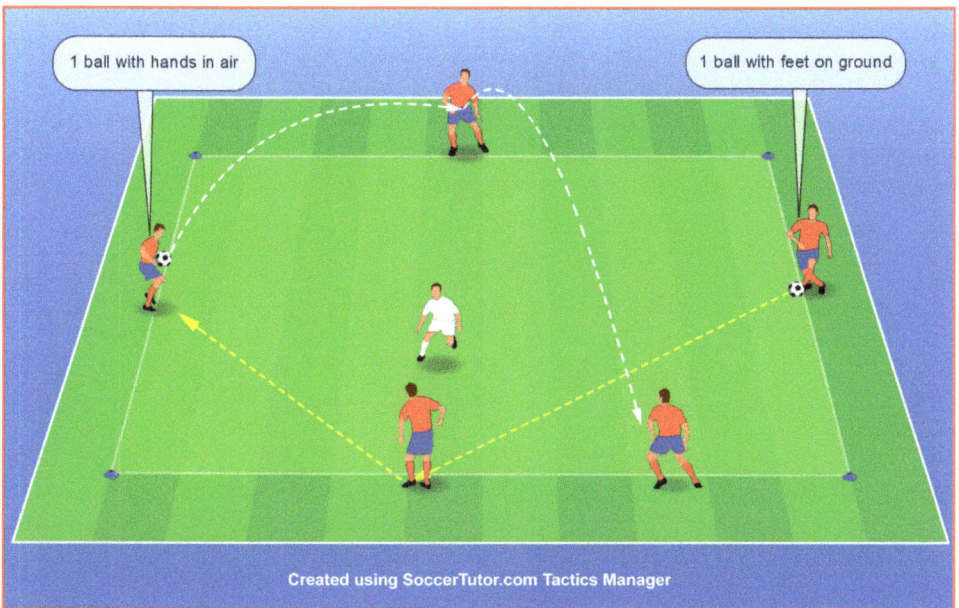

Objective: Quick passing under pressure to maintain possession.

Description

In a 5 x 10 yard area, we have 4/5 outside players and 1 inside player (white). The red outside players try to keep possession for as long as possible, keeping the 2 balls away from the white defender.

We have 2 balls being used at the same time. The first ball is played along the ground with the players using their feet. The second ball is thrown in the air with the players using their hands.

The white defender can use his hands to intercept the second ball which is being thrown, but cannot for the first ball.

If the white defender intercepts a ball (either with his feet or hands), he switches roles with the red outside player who lost possession.

Progressions

1. You can start with 4 players and 1 ball, then progress to 5 players and 2 balls.
2. On the coach's whistle, the ball being passed along the ground with the feet is now thrown in the air using the hands and vice versa - this tests concentration levels.

Chapter 5: Rondos

5 v 2 Rondo with Movement to Switch Sides

8 min

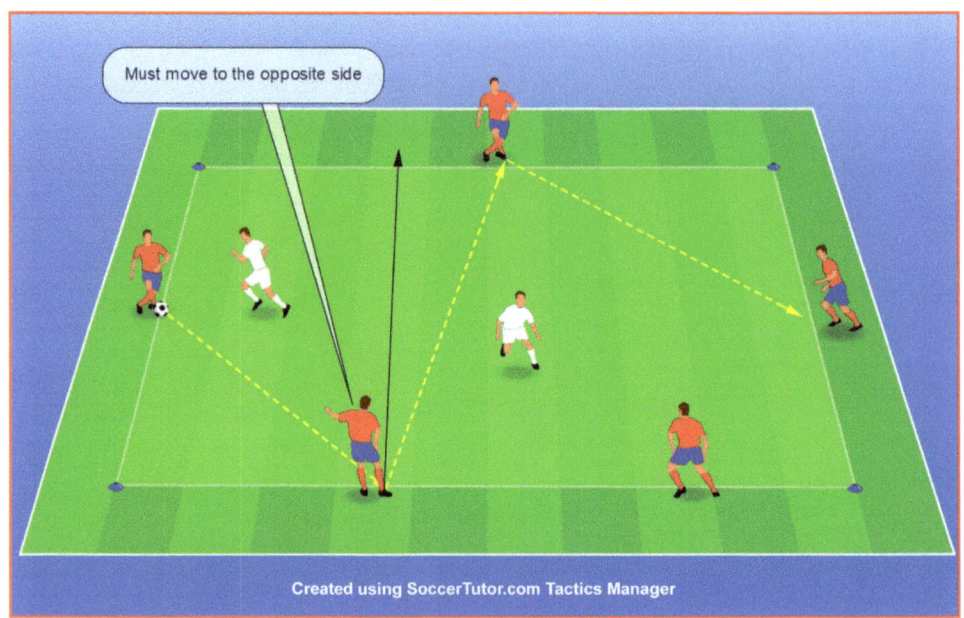

Objective: Quick passing under pressure to maintain possession.

Description

In a 5 x 10 yard area we play a 5 v 2 Rondo.

This is a normal 5 v 2 Rondo with the 5 red players trying to maintain possession and the 2 white defenders trying to intercept the ball.

As there are 5 red players, 2 of them have to be on one side as shown. When one of these players makes a pass, he must then move to the opposite side.

The 2 players on the same side are not allowed to pass to each other. The players use a maximum of 2 touches (control + pass).

Progressions

1. Play "touch and a half" - if a player uses 2 touches, the next player must make a 1 touch pass.
2. Once the players start to maintain possession comfortably, progress to limiting all players to 1 touch.

Chapter 5: Rondos

4 (+1) v 2 Rondo with Inside Player Switching with Outside Players

8 min

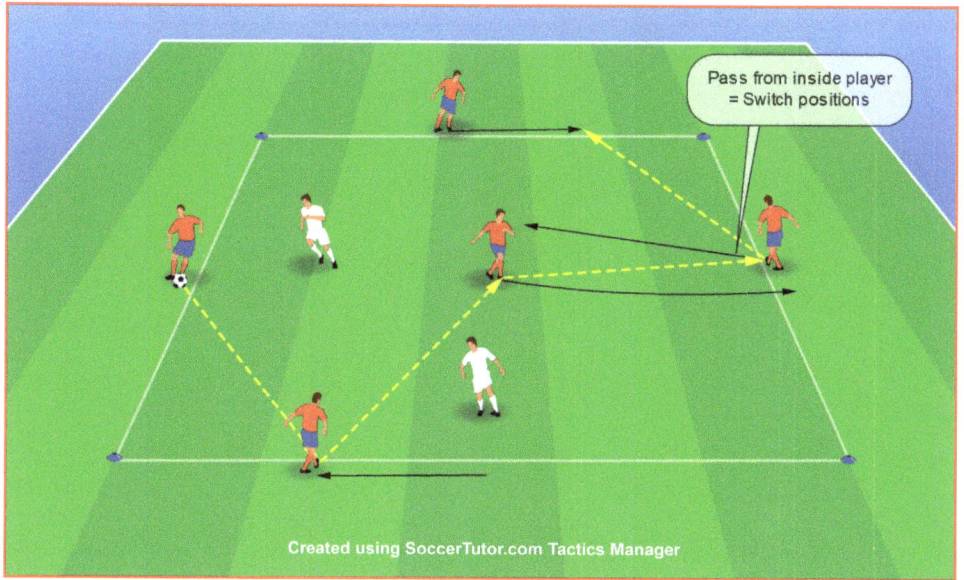

Objective: Passing, receiving in space and possession play.

Description

In a 10 x 10 yard square we again play a 5 v 2 Rondo. There is 1 red player on each side and 1 red player inside. Both white defenders work together inside the square.

The red players try to maintain possession with the focus on finding the red inside player. The inside player must never stand still and should always be providing a passing option for the outside players.

When the inside player receives and then passes to one of the outside players, the 2 players switch positions/roles.

The players have unlimited touches.

Progressions

1. All red players must follow every pass, constantly switching positions with all of their teammates.
2. Once the players start to maintain possession comfortably, progress to limiting all players to 2 touches only.

Chapter 5: Rondos

5 v 2 Rondo "Hit the Middle Cone"

10 min

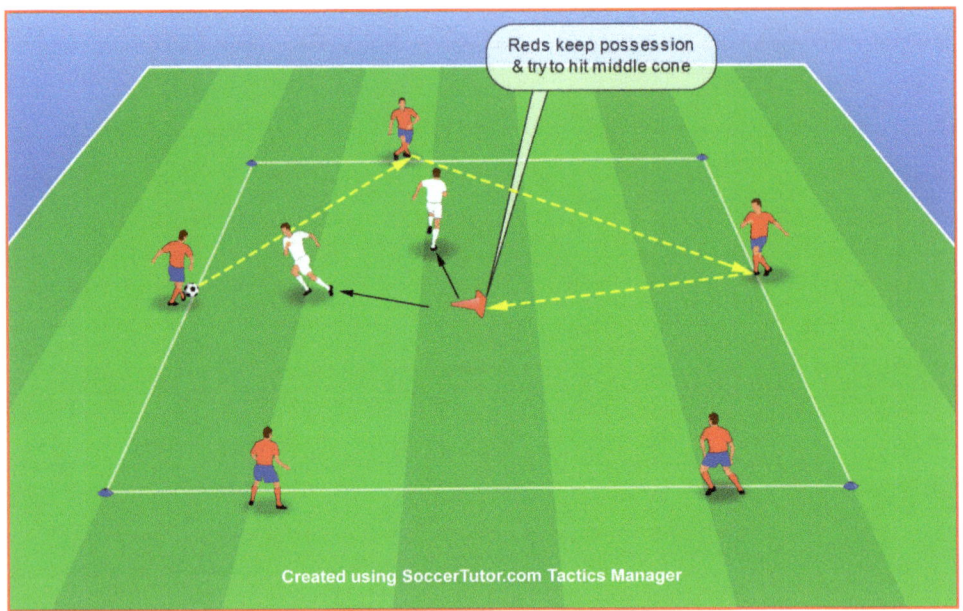

Description

In a 10 yard square, we play a 5 v 2 (or 6 v 2) Rondo. We also have a large cone in the centre which is used as a target. There are 5/6 red players on the outside who try to keep possession against 2 white defenders who have 2 functions:

a. Intercept the ball.

b. Stop the red players from hitting the cone in the centre.

The aim for the red players is to first to keep possession - if they complete 'X' amount of consecutive passes they score 1 point. They also try to hit the central cone at any given opportunity to score 2 points.

Change the roles of the defenders after a set time period or after they have won the ball a certain number of times.

Coaching Point: The inside defending players must communicate and work together, to close the passing angles and the path to the central cone.

Progressions

1. Add another cone to defend.
2. Limit the players to a maximum of 2 touches (control + pass).

Chapter 5: Rondos

4 v 2 Rondos and Speed Exercises

10 min

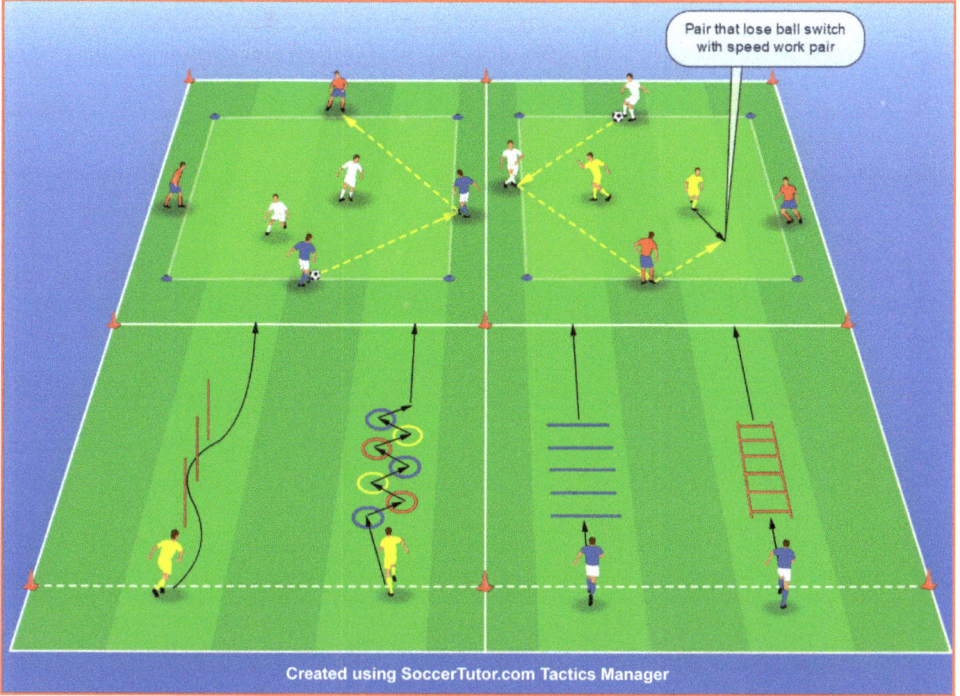

Objective: Quick passing under pressure to maintain possession + speed, agility and coordination.

Description

For this practice, we create 4 squares as shown. We have 4 teams, each with 4 players (2 pairs).

Two pairs (yellow and blue) start in the speed/coordination squares and perform different exercises as shown.

The rest of the players are playing in one of the two 4 v 2 Rondos (8 yard squares).

- When a defending pair win the ball (yellow pair in diagram), they move to the outside of the Rondo.
- The pair that lost the ball (reds in diagram) move to a speed/coordination exercise square and switch roles with the pair that are in there (who become the defenders in the Rondo).

The practice is continuous with the pairs switching roles. Allow rest time.

Chapter 5: Rondos

Changing 4 v 1 Rondo Positions with Support Play in 4 Squares

10 min

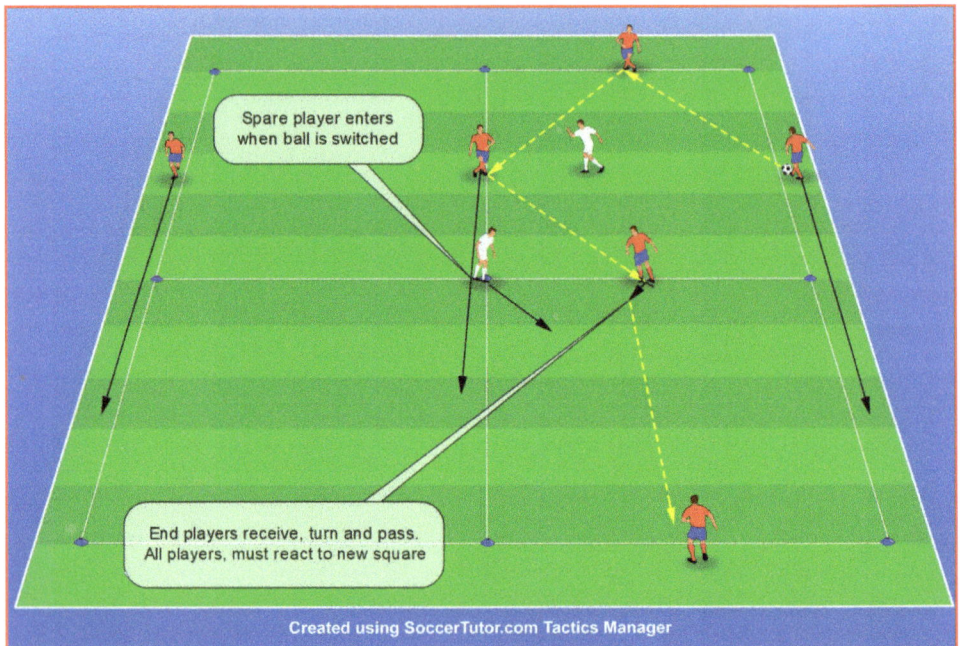

Description

Mark out four 8 yard squares as shown. We have 6 red players in total and 2 white defenders. We start in one of the squares with a 4 v 1 Rondo. The red players try to maintain possession and the white player tries to intercept the ball.

When one of the red players who is joined to another square receives, he can turn and pass to the teammate waiting in that square. All the red players (except for one) move across to play a 4 v 1 Rondo in that square.

The spare white player enters the new square after the ball is switched. The other white player becomes spare and waits.

This is a dynamic practice with all the players having to react quickly to the changing situations. If a defender touches the ball, he swaps roles with one of the red players. After the ball has been passed to 3-5 different squares without a defender touching it, one of the defenders becomes an attacker automatically.

Variations

1. Only allow 2 touches for the end players when they turn and pass to another square. The other players have 1 touch.
2. Start with only 2 zones. Both defenders are in the middle holding hands.

Chapter 5: Rondos

Transition from Attack to Defence in Simultaneous 4 v 1 Rondos

10 min

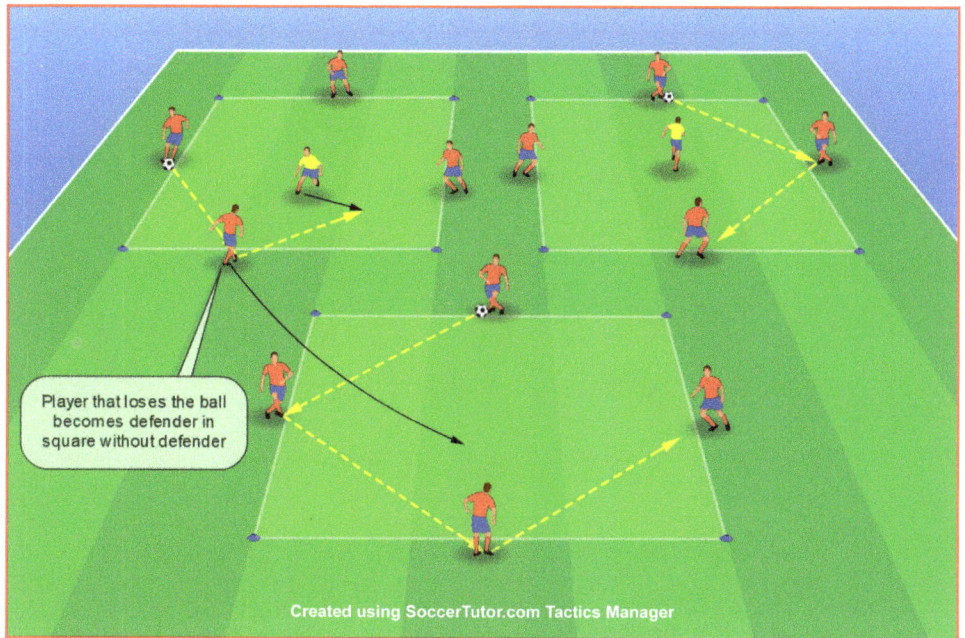

Player that loses the ball becomes defender in square without defender

Objective: Quick passing under pressure to maintain possession and quick reactions.

Description

In this practice, we mark out three 8 yard squares with 1 player on each side, as shown.

In two of the squares, we have an active 4 v 2 Rondo and in the third there is no defender. In the third square, the players simply keep the ball moving, passing to one another.

When one of the defenders (yellow bib) wins the ball in an active Rondo, he then moves to the outside. The player that lost the ball takes the yellow bib and runs to the empty Rondo to become the defender in there.

The practice is continuous.

Variation: Allow the players to run into an active Rondo that already has a defender to create a 4 v 2 situation.

Progression: Limit the players to a maximum of 2 touches.

©SoccerTutor.com *Spanish Football Federation Coaching*

Chapter 5: Rondos

End to End 4 (+3) v 4 Rondo

8 min

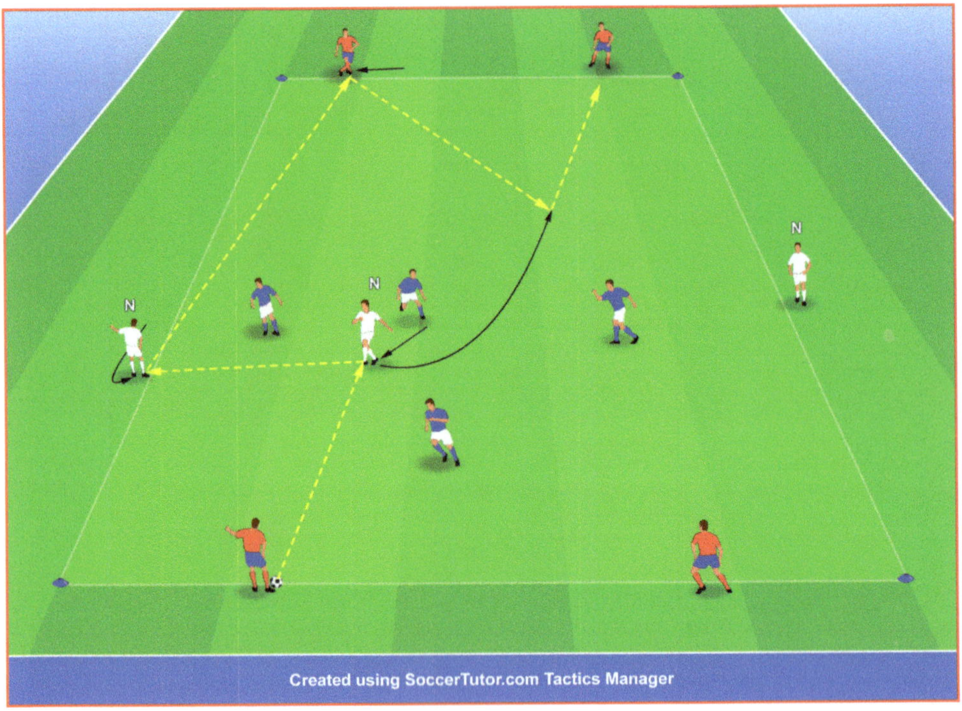

Objective: Passing and support/possession play.

Description

In a 20 x 30 yard area, we have 2 teams (4 players each) and 3 neutral players. One team (red) starts with 2 players outside at each end. The other team (blue) have all of their players inside. We have 2 white neutral players outside at the sides and 1 inside.

The practice starts with one of the red players on the outside and the red team try to keep possession with the help of the neutral players, as shown. This works as a 7 v 4 Rondo. The focus should be on moving the ball from one end to the other and vice versa.

If the blue team win the ball, they switch roles with the red team and move to the outside. The red team move inside and now defend in the same 7 v 4 situation.

Variations

1. Change the positioning so that there is 1 neutral player at each end. The team in possession then have 2 players on each side.
2. The neutral players can only use their weaker foot.

CHAPTER 6

Possession Games

Chapter 6: Possession Games

POSSESSION TRAINING METHODOLOGY

- Possession training is used to create a noticeable improvement in the collective game of the team, as you can see in the practices that we present in this chapter.

- The players must learn to pass under pressure, receive in space and make supporting movements for their teammates.

- With younger players, we perform the practices with defenders holding hands. This makes it much more difficult to win the ball, so the attacking players have more success at passing and keeping possession.

- We make sure that developing players get plenty of time on the ball, acquiring a trust and confidence that until that moment many do not have.

- Once the players are more developed technically, we can relax these restrictions and allow them to play more freely in our possession practices with active defenders.

- The practices presented in this chapter are used with our U9-12 players at the RFEF Coaching School - you can increase/decrease the difficulty level with simple variations.

Chapter 6: Possession Games

Possession Game with Increasing Opposition (5 v 1 to 5 v 5)

10 min

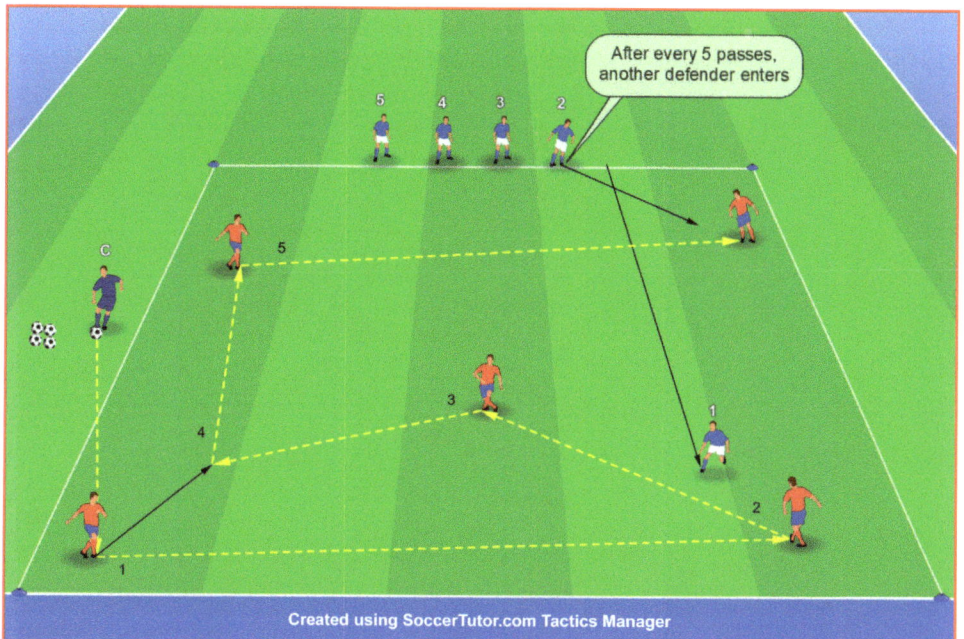

Description

We mark out a square suitable for the age/level of the players and we have 2 teams of 5 players. One team (red) starts inside the area and the other team (blue) stand outside on one side - they are numbered 1-5 as shown.

The practice starts when the coach passes to a red player. As soon as this happens, blue No.1 moves inside to press. We have a 5 v 1 situation and the reds try to keep possession. The blue player's aim is to win the ball or kick it out of play.

After the red team have completed 5 passes, the next blue player moves inside to apply pressure. Every 5 passes we go from 5 v 2 -> 5 v 3 -> 5 v 4 -> 5 v 5.

If the reds complete 5 passes in a 5 v 5 situation, they score 2 points. If the blue team win the ball (1 point), the coach passes a new ball in and the practice starts again from the beginning with a 5 v 1 situation.

Halfway through the practice, change the team roles.

Variations

1. Change the number of passes to be completed before the next player enters.
2. Limit the number of touches the red players are allowed.

Chapter 6: Possession Games

Three Team 4 (+4) v 4 Possession Game

10-15 min

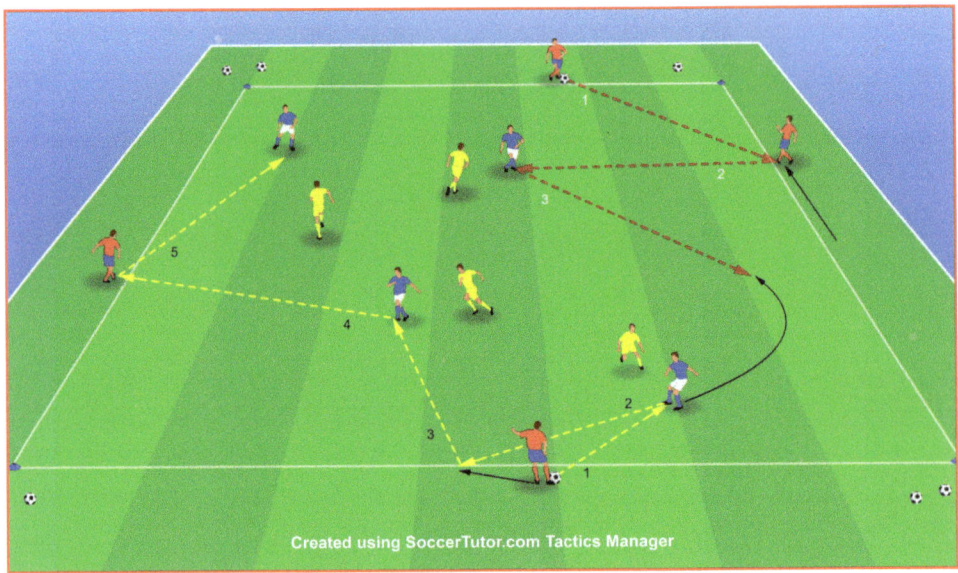

Objective: Passing, receiving in space, support and possession play.

Description

Using an area suitable for the age/level of the players, we have 3 teams with 4 players each. Two teams have all their players on the inside and the red team are on the outside with 1 player on each side.

We start with 2 balls from the outside. One team (reds) and another team (blues) try to maintain possession in an 8 v 4 situation against the yellows.

The outside players (reds) are limited to 1 touch, so the inside players (blues) must quickly provide support to receive back.

After a set amount of time, change the roles of the teams. The team that wins the ball the most times wins.

Variation

To make keeping possession easier, you can have the defending team form 2 pairs that hold hands.

Support Play in an 8 v 6 Possession Game

10-12 min

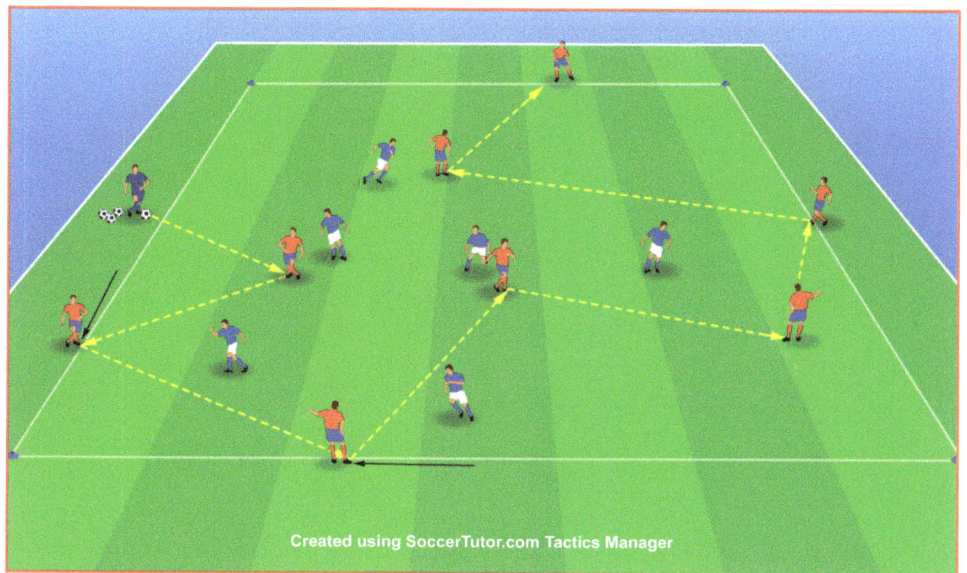

Objective: Passing, receiving in space, support and possession play.

Description

Using an area suitable for the age/level of the players, we have 2 teams.

The red team have 8 players - 4 inside and 4 outside as shown in the diagram. The blue team defend with 6 players who are all inside the area.

The practice starts with the coach's pass to an inside red player, as shown in the diagram.

We have an 8 v 4 situation and the aim is to maintain possession and complete a set amount of consecutive passes e.g. 8 passes = 1 point.

If the blue defending team win the ball or kick it out of play, they score 1 point.

Play for a set period of time and then change the defenders.

Progressions

1. Play "touch and a half" - if a player uses 2 touches, the next player must make a 1 touch pass.
2. Once the players start to maintain possession comfortably, progress to limiting all players to 1 touch.

Possession Game with Players Switching Inside / Outside

6-8 min

Objective: Passing, receiving, switching positions and possession play.

Description

Using an area suitable for the age/level of the players, we have 2 teams of 6 players. Each team has 4 players inside the area and 2 players on opposite sides, as shown.

The practice starts with the coach's pass inside. The team in possession use the outside players so we have a 6 v 4 situation.

The aim is to keep possession and pass to the outside players. Each time this happens, the player who makes the pass and the outside player interchange positions (1 point).

The outside player can either receive and dribble inside or pass inside to continue the practice. If the defending team (blues) win the ball, they have the same aims.

Variations

1. Allow the 2 outside players to move around the whole square when their team are in possession - they don't have to just remain on one side.
2. To make keeping possession easier, you can have the defending players inside the area form 2 pairs that hold hands.

Chapter 6: Possession Games

Three Team Possession Game with Receiving Corners

3 x 4 min

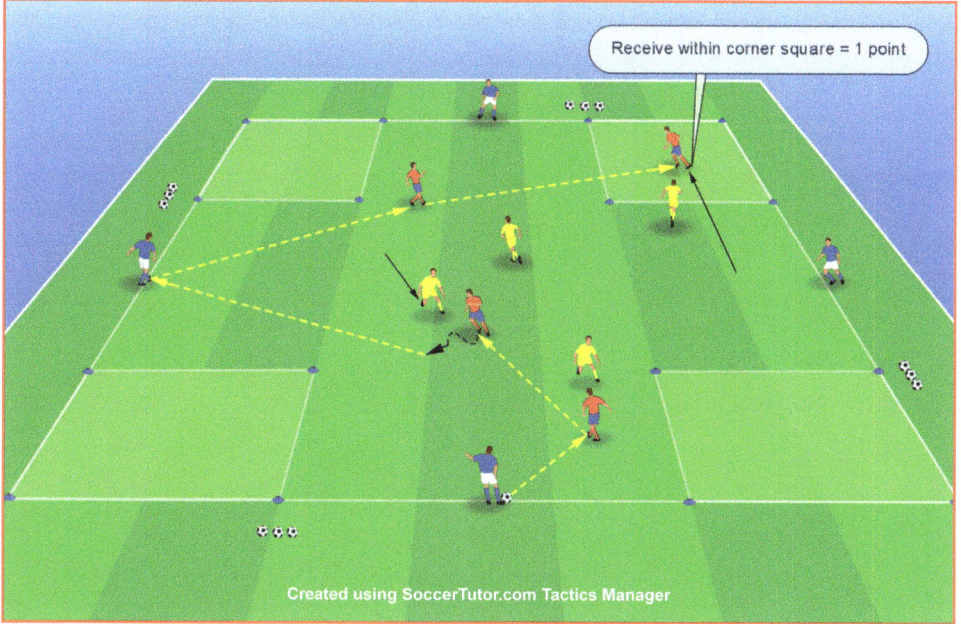

Objective: Passing, receiving in space, support and possession play.

Description

Using an area suitable for the age/level of the players, we mark out 4 corner zones as shown. We have 3 teams, each with 4 players. One team (blue) has a player positioned on each side and the other 2 teams have all of their players inside.

A blue outside player starts the practice by passing to an inside player - that team (reds in diagram) then have an 8 v 4 situation (with help from blues) and try to first keep possession, and then receive within one of the corner zones to score 1 point.

If the defending team (yellows) win the ball, they then become the attacking team with an 8 v 4 situation and the same aims. Swap the team roles so the blues move inside after a set amount of time.

Coaching Point: Encourage mobility and support for the ball carrier at all times.

Variations

1. Players are not allowed inside the corner zones until a pass has been made - they must then time their movement to receive within the corner zone.
2. The teams can only receive within 2 corner zones (diagonally opposite), which means they defend the other 2.

©SoccerTutor.com   *Spanish Football Federation Coaching*

Chapter 6: Possession Games

Possession Play in a 2 Zone Transition Game

10 min

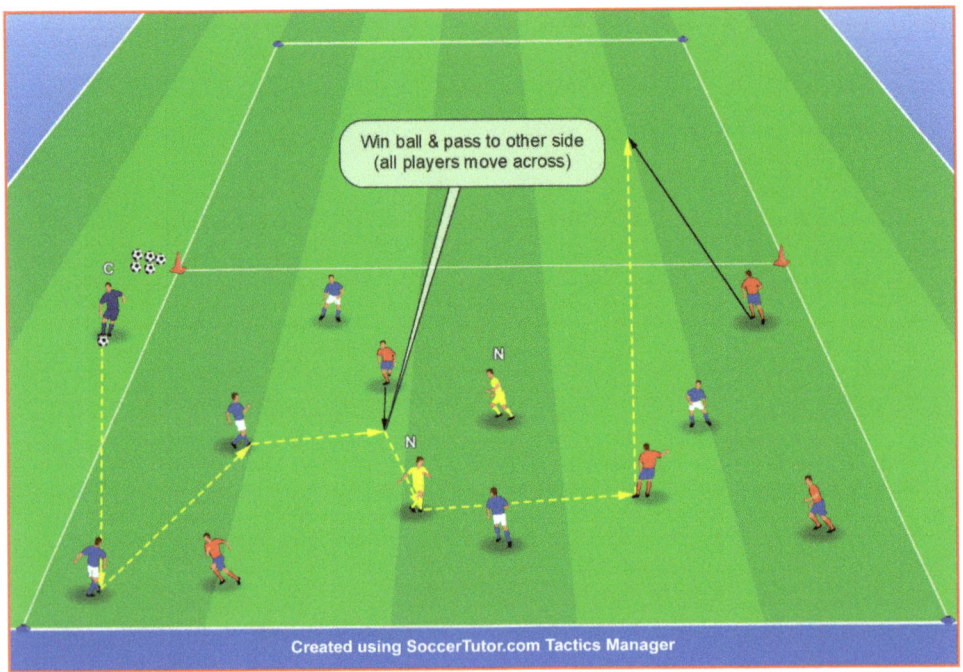

Description

Using an area suitable for the age/level of the players, we mark out 2 equal zones. All of the players start in one zone - we have 2 teams of 5 players and 2 extra yellow neutral players who play with the team in possession.

The practice starts with the coach's pass inside to one team (blues in diagram). They aim to keep possession in a 7 v 5 situation (with help from the yellow neutral players).

The defending team (reds in diagram) try to win the ball - when they do their aim is to pass into the other zone (quick transition). All players move across and the reds now have a 7 v 5 situation, trying to keep possession. The blues try to win the ball and then perform the same transition in the opposite direction.

If a team wins the ball and then loses it again before making the transition, the practice continues with a 7 v 5 situation in that zone.

Variations

1. You can have 1 or 2 players from the defending team waiting for a pass in the other zone, and have a 7 v 4 or 7 v 3 situation in the first zone.
2. Depending on the level of the players, you can start by playing with the hands.

Chapter 6: Possession Games

Retain the Ball and Switch Play in a Two Sided Possession Game

8 min

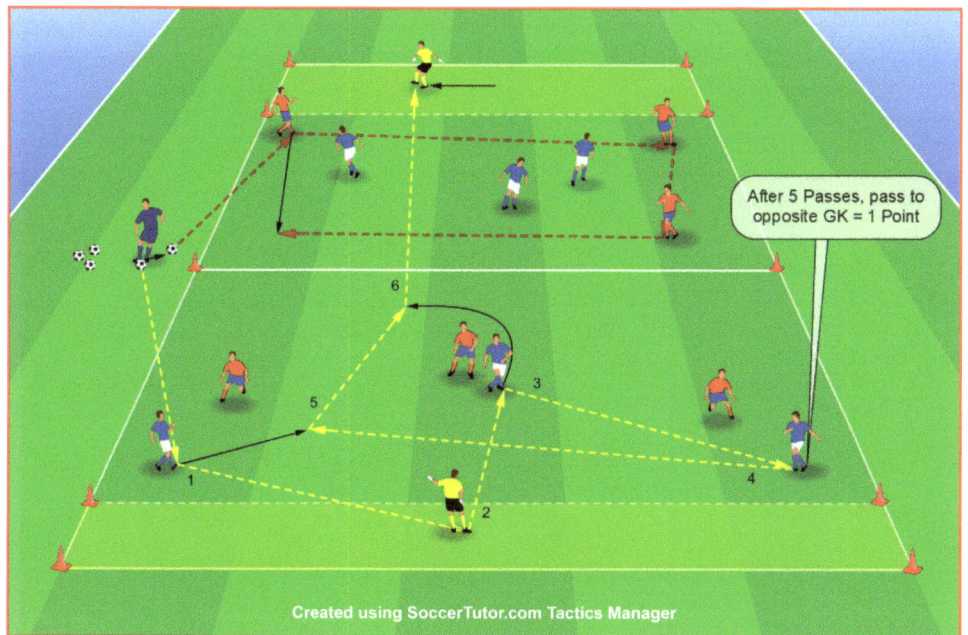

Objective: To practice possession and transition play in a dynamic game.

Description

In a 20 x 30 yard area, we have two 3 v 3 situations that are played simultaneously. We also have 2 extra 5 yard zones at the ends with goalkeepers who act as neutral players to help teams retain possession.

The coach starts the practice by passing 2 balls in - 1 into each zone. The aim for the team in possession is to complete 5 consecutive passes and then pass to the goalkeeper at the opposite end - if he receives successfully within his end zone, the team score 1 point.

If the defending team win the ball, they become the attackers with the same aims. All players are limited to a maximum of 2 touches throughout.

Variations

1. The coach shouts out a colour and the players on that team must all switch zones right away, moving to defend and try to win the ball.
2. Each time a player scores a point by passing across to the opposite goalkeeper, he then moves into the zone on that side. The practice then constantly has changes in superiority and inferiority of numbers in each zone.

Chapter 6: Possession Games

Possession and Switching Play in a Three Team Zonal Game

10 min

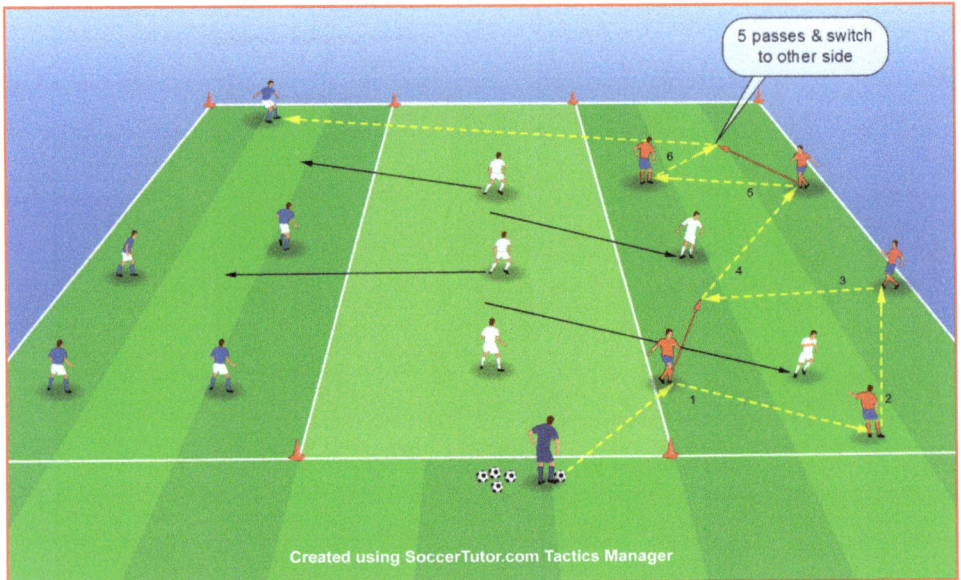

Objective: Passing, receiving in space, support play and possession play.

Description

Using an area suitable for the age/level of the players, we mark out 3 equal zones as shown in the diagram. There are 3 teams of 5 players - we start with the blue and red teams in the end zones, and the white team in the middle zone.

The coach starts the practice by passing to a team in an end zone (reds in diagram) - 2 white players move across to create a 5 v 2 situation.

The aim for the red team is to complete 5 passes and then pass to the blue team in the other end zone - they must be careful this pass is not intercepted by any of the 3 white players in the middle zone. At this point, 2 white players from the middle zone move across to create the same 5 v 2 situation and the practice continues.

If the white team win the ball, they then pass to the other end and switch roles with the team that lost the ball.

Variations

1. Depending on the difficulty level, you can allow the middle 3 players to intercept the pass from one end zone to another, or not.
2. Allow 3 players to move from the middle zone to create a 5 v 3 situation in the end zone.

Chapter 6: Possession Games

Possession Game with Quick Reaction Sprints

8-10 min

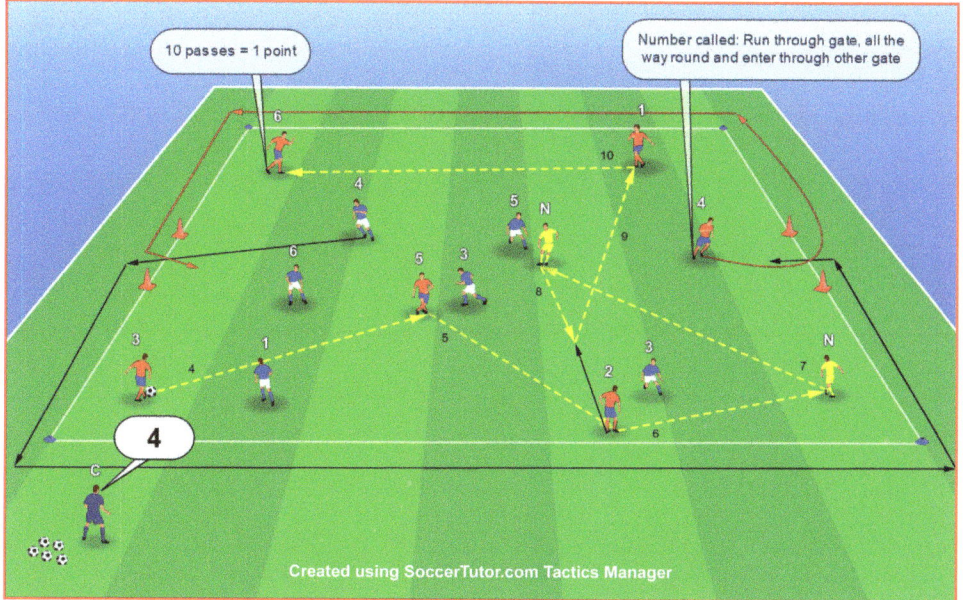

Objective: Passing, receiving, support, possession play and quick reactions/speed.

Description

Using an area suitable for the age/level of the players, we have 2 teams with 6 players each - they are numbered 1-6 as shown in the diagram. We also have 2 neutral players who play with the team in possession to create an 8 v 6 situation.

The practice starts with the coach's pass inside. The aim is to maintain possession and complete a set amount of consecutive passes e.g. 8-10 passes = 1 point.

Every 30 seconds, the coach calls out a number - the players called (No.4 in diagram) must run through one of the cone gates, all the way around the pitch and back through the other cone gate. It is a race, so the first player to get back inside scores 1 point. The rest of the players continue to play, trying to complete 8-10 passes.

All players are limited to 2 touches.

Progressions

1. Play "touch and a half" - if a player uses 2 touches, the next player must make a 1 touch pass.
2. Once the players start to maintain possession comfortably, progress to playing an equal 7 v 7 game.

CHAPTER 7

Heading

Chapter 7: Heading

HEADING TRAINING METHODOLOGY

- In many cases, coaches don't use much time training heading. They may do a little bit of heading practice or incorporate some heading into practices focussing on other technical aspects.

- At the RFEF Coaching School, we make time to train heading with specifically designed practices.

- The players learn how to control the ball using their head, pass using their head and finish using their head.

- However, most of the practices incorporate other elements to make it more game realistic i.e. Movement, pass, shoot etc.

Chapter 7: Heading

Headed Pass + Compete in the Air in a Continuous Circuit Warm Up

10 min

Objective: Controlled heading and jumping to compete in the air.

Description

Using a large area, we have 8 different feeder stations marked by the red cones and a central circle area, as shown. In this example we have 16 players - if you have less players, just have less feeder stations.

- By each red cone we have a blue player with a ball in his hands. The red players do not have balls and move around the stations in an anti-clockwise direction.
- At each station, the blue player throws the ball up and the red player heads it back.
- After each station, the red players run to the central circle to compete with one teammate - they jump up in the air, making contact as if competing for a header. They then move to the next station and continue the practice.
- The red players perform 2/3 series (1 -> 8) and then switch roles with the blue players.

Variations

1. The red players can control with the head and then volley back.
2. When the red players head the ball back, the blue player must control the ball with his chest, thigh or feet.

Chapter 7: Heading

'Score Only with Headers' in a 7 v 7 Warm Up Game

15 min

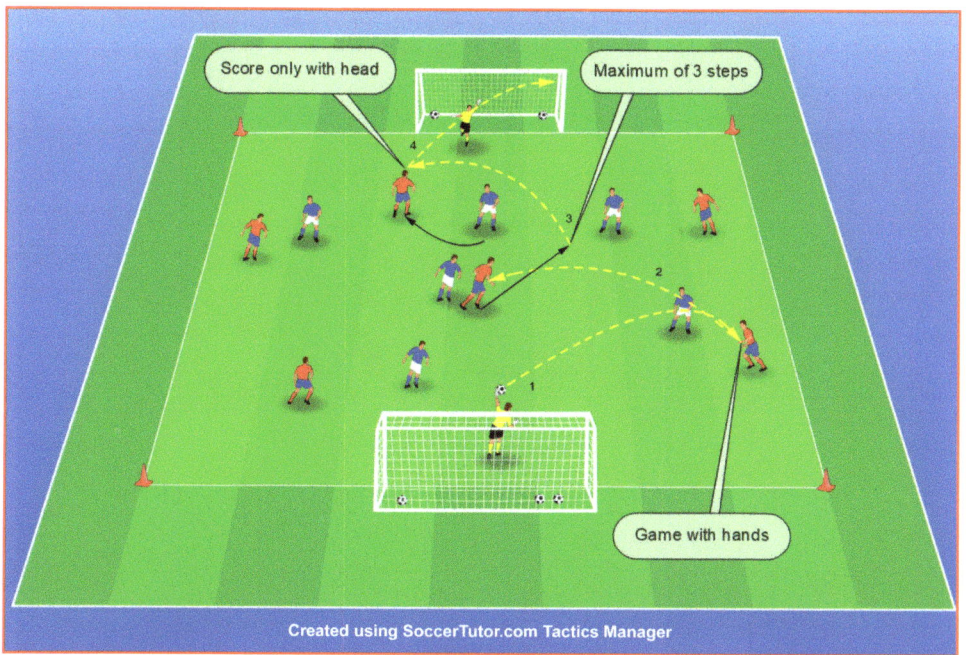

Description

In a 20 x 20 yard area, we play a 7 v 7 game.

The practice starts with one of the goalkeepers and the players throw the ball to each other, playing only with their hands and heads. The only way to score is with the head.

When in possession of the ball with the hands, players can only take a maximum of 3 steps.

Defenders are not allowed to intercept a header with their hands - only their body or head, unless the ball touches the ground first.

Variations

1. If a team scores after 2 consecutive touches with the head, the goal is worth double.
2. Players pass with their feet. They still receive with their hands and finish with their head.
3. Play with 2 balls at once.

Chapter 7: Heading

Backwards Headers Relay Race

6-8 min

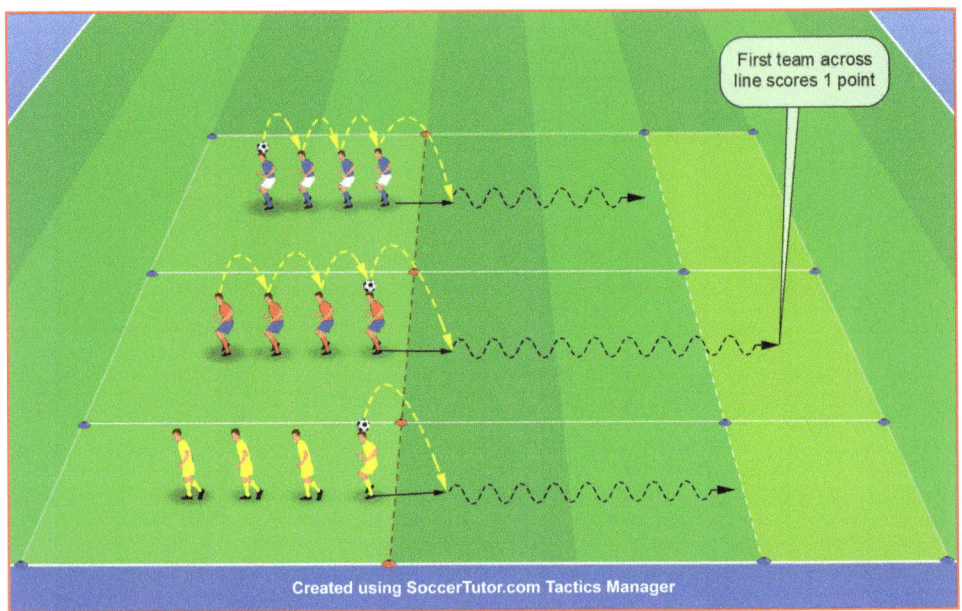

Objective: Headed control and touch with dribbling at speed.

Description

This is a very simple practice - we have 3 teams with 4 players each in their own channel. The players stand close together, facing one way, as shown in the diagram.

The 3 teams compete in this race. The first player heads the ball up and back to the second player. The players can only use their heads and must pass the ball backwards along the line.

The fourth player heads the ball back, turns and then dribbles into the end zone, as shown. The team that dribbles the ball into the end zone first scores 1 point.

You can allow the players to have unlimited touches with the head if necessary and progress to only 1 touch per player allowed.

Variation

Position the players in a zig-zag formation - they then must head the ball at a backwards diagonal angle through the 4 players.

Chapter 7: Heading

Consecutive Header Team Game

8 min

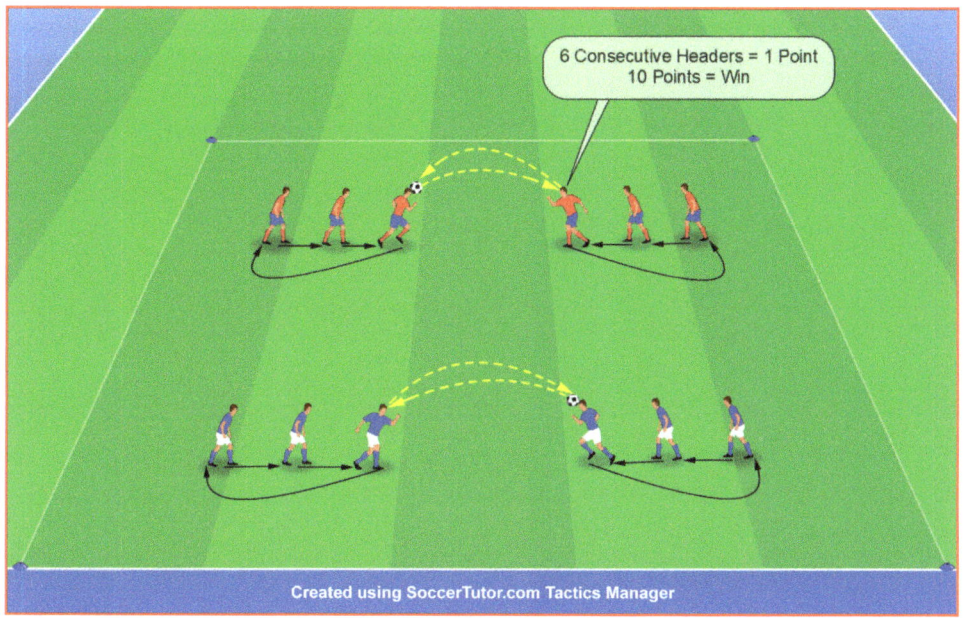

Objective: Accurate headed passing.

Description

We split the players into 2 teams. Each team is split in half with the players facing other, as shown in the diagram.

The practice starts with the first player throwing the ball up and heading to his teammate opposite who heads the ball back.

After heading the ball, the player moves to the back of the line and the next player moves forward to head next.

If a team completes 6 consecutive headers, then they score 1 point. The first team to score 10 points wins.

Variations

1. After heading, the player runs at maximum speed to the back of the opposite line.
2. Add a passive defender in front of the lines to make the heading more difficult.

Chapter 7: Heading

Competing for Headers at Different Angles and Heights

8 min

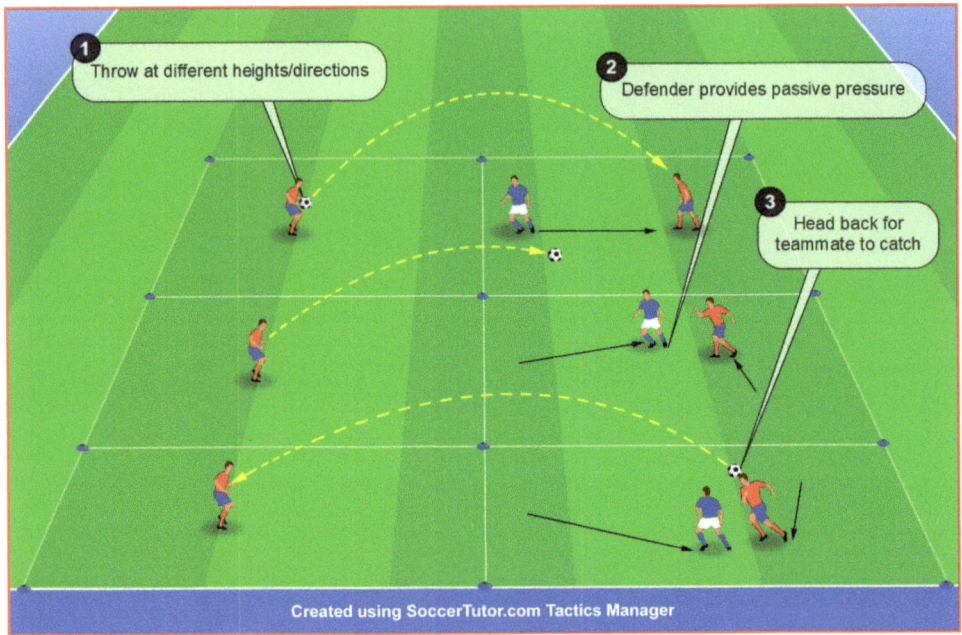

Objective: Judging the flight of the ball, competing in the air and winning headers.

Description

For this practice we work in groups of 3 in channels. We have 1 red player on each side and a blue player in the middle.

The practice starts with a red player throwing the ball in the air - the throw varies each time to provide different heights and directions.

The blue player moves backwards to apply passive pressure, as the red player tries to head the ball back for his teammate to catch.

Each player performs the practice for 1 minute or performs 4 repetitions. After this, the players rotate their roles and positions.

Progressions

1. Make the blue defender fully active - he challenges the red player and tries to head the ball away.
2. Throw 10 balls with a fully active defender. The red and blue players compete and get a point each time they win the header.

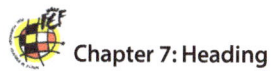
Chapter 7: Heading

Resistance, Sprint + Headed Finish

3 x 4 min

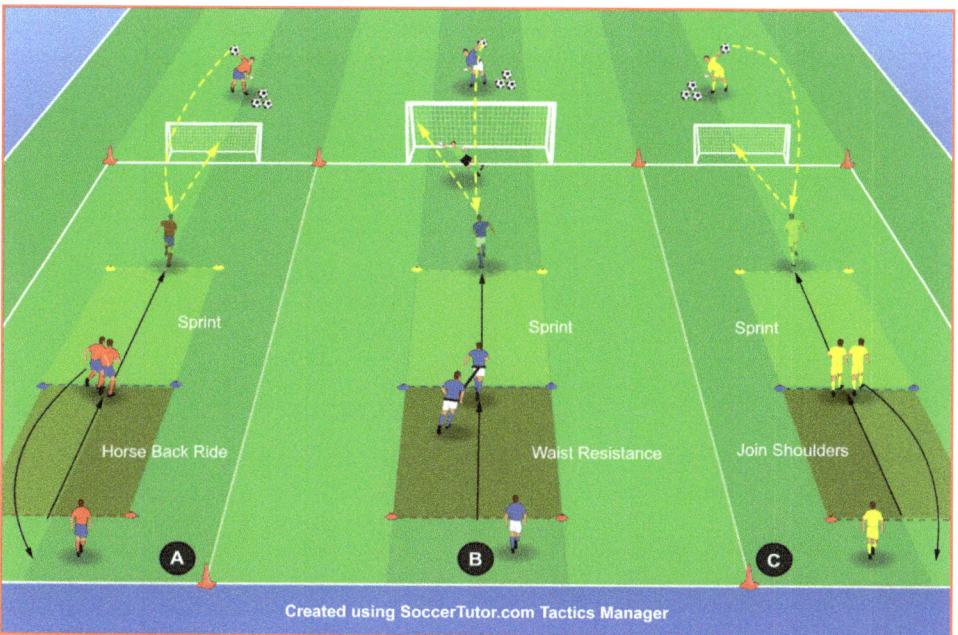

Description

In a 40 x 30 yard area, we mark out 3 different zones as shown. The zones at the sides (A & C) are 10 x 30 yards and the middle zone is 20 x 30 yards:

A. The first red player has to carry a teammate on this back for 10 yards (horseback ride), then sprints forward 10 yards. The teammate outside the area throws a ball in and the player must head the ball into the small goal.

B. The blue player has to move forward with a teammate holding or attached to his waist (resistance) for 10 yards, then sprints forward 10 yards. The teammate outside the area throws a ball in and the player tries to score with a header past the GK.

C. The yellow player has to move forward joined at the shoulders to a teammate (resistance) for 10 yards, then sprints forward 10 yards. The teammate outside the area throws a ball in and the player must head the ball into the small goal.

Teams get 1 point for every goal scored. The player that heads at goal moves to the thrower's position, the thrower moves to the start and the next player goes.

Progression

The second player who provides the resistance in the first part (horseback ride, waist resistance or join shoulders) then becomes a defender when the player tries to score.

Chapter 7: Heading

Hand + Header Game / Sprint, Hurdle + Header / Chip + Header

3 x 2 min

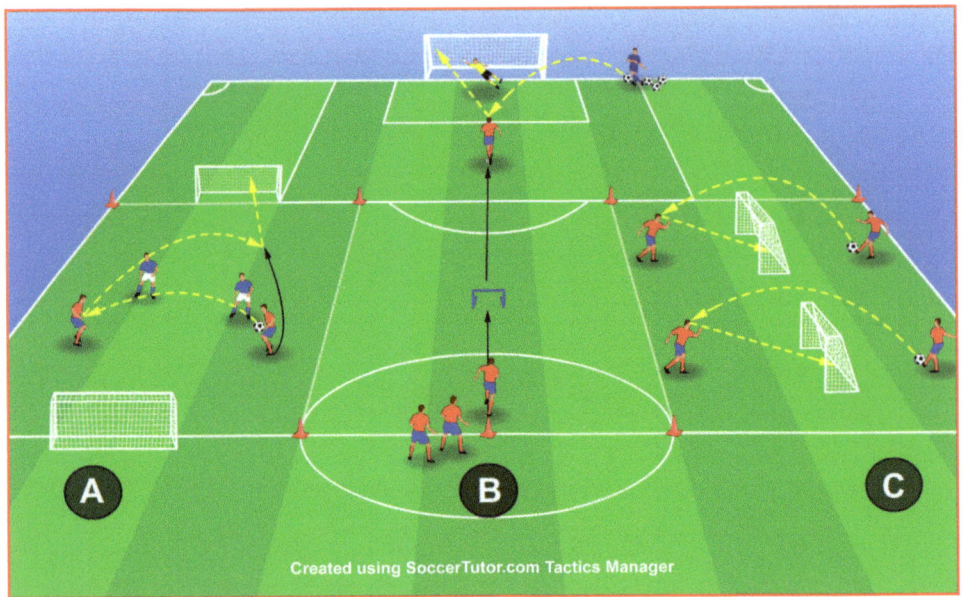

Objective: Headed passing and finishing.

Description

Using half a youth pitch, we create 3 zones (A, B & C), as shown in the diagram.

Within each zone we have 4 players. We also have a goal with a goalkeeper and a coach with lots of footballs.

A. This is a 2 v 2 game with small goals. The team in possession (reds) play with their hands and heads. They can only score with a headed finish. The defenders can use any part of their body except their hands to try to intercept the ball.

B. The players run forward, jump over the hurdle and then sprint into the penalty area. The coach throws or chips the ball up for the player to try and head it past the goalkeeper.

C. The players are in pairs - one player chips the ball up over the goal and the second player tries to head the ball into the goal. Each player gets 3 attempts before they switch roles.

Variation: Within each group, 2 pairs can compete to see who scores the most points.

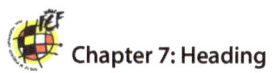
Chapter 7: Heading

Sprint + Headed Finish / 3 v 3 Hands and Headers Game

2 x 6 min

Description

For this practice, we run two practices at the same time:

1. For the first practice, we have 6 players. One of the players acts as a goalkeeper and the other players are behind the cones as shown. The first player runs forward and tries to score with a header from the coach's throw.

   Every time the player in the goal manages to make a save (or the attacker misses), he switches roles with the player who failed to score. If the player scores with a header, he goes back to the start position. The practice is continuous.

2. The second group play a 3 v 3 game with small goals - they play with their hands and heads. For a goal to count, there must be at least 1 header in the build-up and they must score with a headed finish.

Variation

For the first practice, the player in the goal will act as a defender and can intercept the ball with any part of the body, except the hands.

Chapter 7: Heading

Headed Passes and Quick Break Away with Finish

10 min

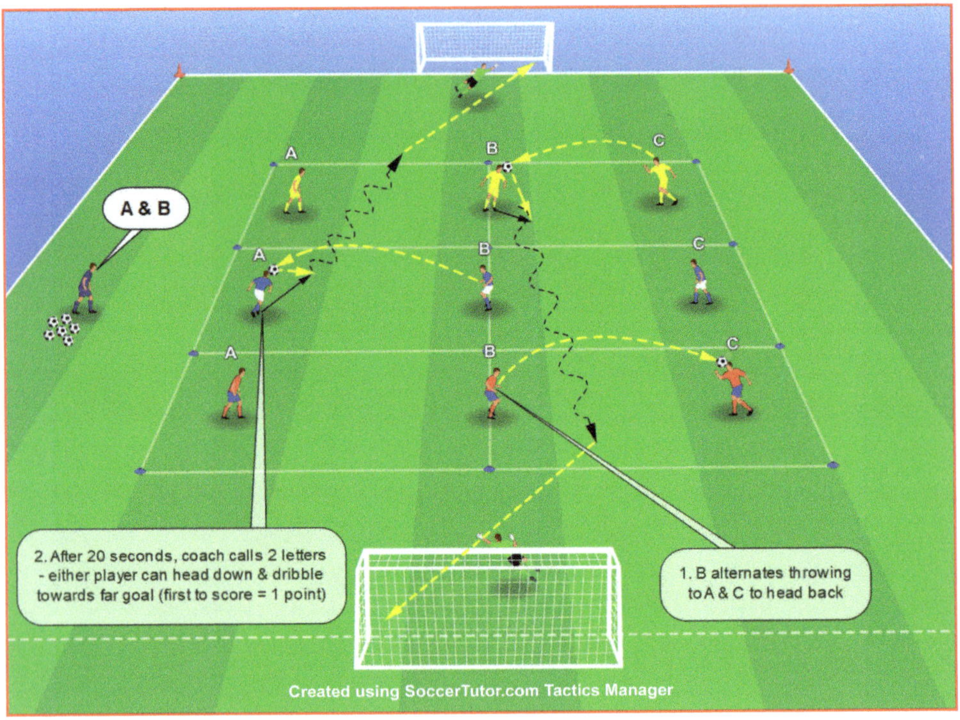

1. B alternates throwing to A & C to head back

2. After 20 seconds, coach calls 2 letters - either player can head down & dribble towards far goal (first to score = 1 point)

Description

In a 50 x 50 yard area, we have a goal with a goalkeeper at both ends - we also mark out a 30 x 30 yard square in the middle which is split into 3 channels, as shown.

1. The players are in groups of 3 with 2 on each side (A & C) and 1 in the middle (B). B alternates throwing the ball up for his 2 teammates, who head the ball back.

2. After 20/30 seconds, the coach calls out 2 letters, for example "A and B" - whichever of these players (in all 3 groups) receives the ball first, controls it and dribbles at maximum speed to the furthest goal to try and score. The first player to score wins a point for his team.

The practice then continues in the same way but we change the Player B role in all 3 groups.

Variations

1. The player whose letter isn't called out can defend to stop the other teams scoring.
2. The players must control with the head before being able to dribble and shoot.

Chapter 7: Heading

Connected 2 Zone Duels with Headers + Counter Attacks

12 min

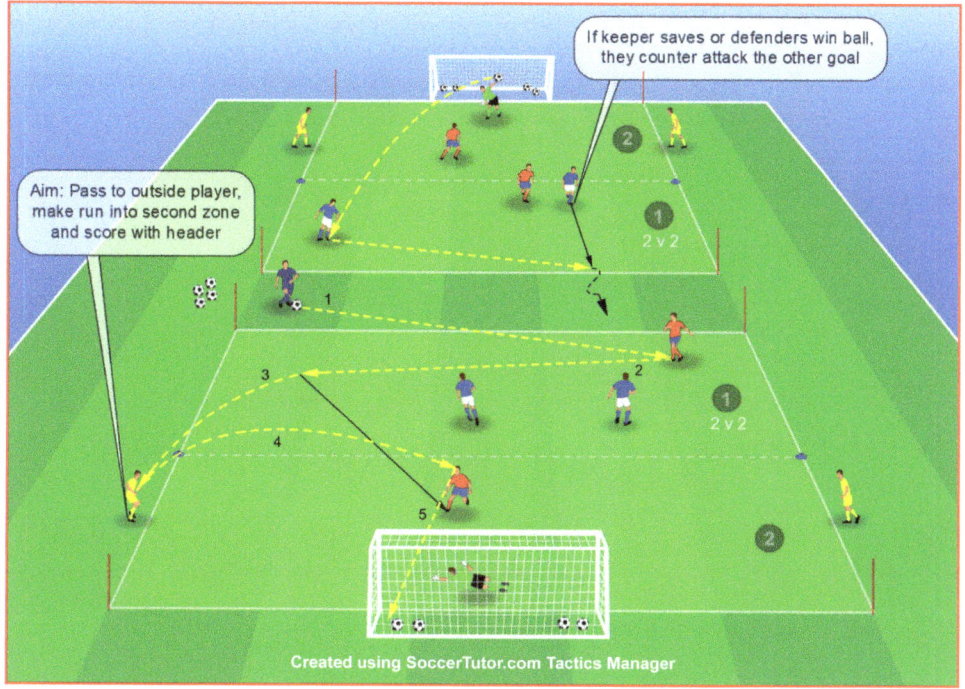

Objective: Headed finishing within a quick counter attack practice.

Description

For this practice we set up 2 games which run at the same time. Both areas are split into 2 equal sized zones and we have a 2 v 2 game + 2 neutral players at the sides. There are also large goals with goalkeepers.

The practice starts when the coach passes to a red player in the first zone where there is a 2 v 2 situation. The aim is to pass the ball into the arms of one of the yellow neutral side players. From this point, the red players can then move into the second zone. The neutral player throws the ball for the red player to score with a header.

If the goalkeeper saves or the blues win the ball in the first zone, the blue team then counter attack in the opposite direction - they attack while trying to evade the other game that is being played at the opposite end and try to score.

Variation

1/2 defenders can enter to defend the header making a 2 v 1 or 2 v 2 in the final zone.

Chapter 7: Heading

Hands + Headers Small Sided Game with Delivery from Wide Players

8-10 min

Objective: Headed passing and finishing.

Description

Using an area double the size of a youth penalty box, we have a 5 v 5 game with 2 extra yellow neutral players at the sides.

- The game starts with a pass from the goalkeeper, who throws the ball out to the head of a player.
- The attacking team (reds) use their head and hands only but they are not allowed to use their hands twice in a row - if the ball is thrown, the next player must head it. For a goal to be scored, it must be with the head.
- The yellow side players are neutral players that catch the ball when they are passed the ball (they can also receive from the goalkeeper). They then throw the ball to an inside player's head.
- The defending team (blues) try to win the ball and then become the attacking team. They can only use their hands to catch the ball if it has been thrown.

Variation

Match players up with an opponent so everybody marks one player, and competes in the air with them throughout.

CHAPTER 8

Finishing

Chapter 8: Finishing

FINISHING TRAINING METHODOLOGY

- The actions of batting to goal and then finishing are repeated many times throughout our training.

- We use progressive training based on repetition, making sure the players are given many opportunities to finish on goal.

- We focus on the execution of the touch before shooting. The touch should be towards goal or at an angle to evade a defender.

- The last touch needs to be with the right force, so the ball is out in front but doesn't go too far away.

- The players need to also learn to use different parts of the foot for the last touch and for finishing.

- One of the premises that we use in the RFEF Coaching School is that once the player is approaching the goalkeeper, they should "PASS AT GOAL". The ball should not be kicked hard, but instead placed in the net far from the goalkeeper. The finish will then be smoother and more accurate.

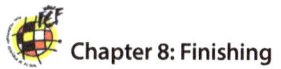

Chapter 8: Finishing

Dribble / Sprint Exercises + Finishing

3 x 3 min

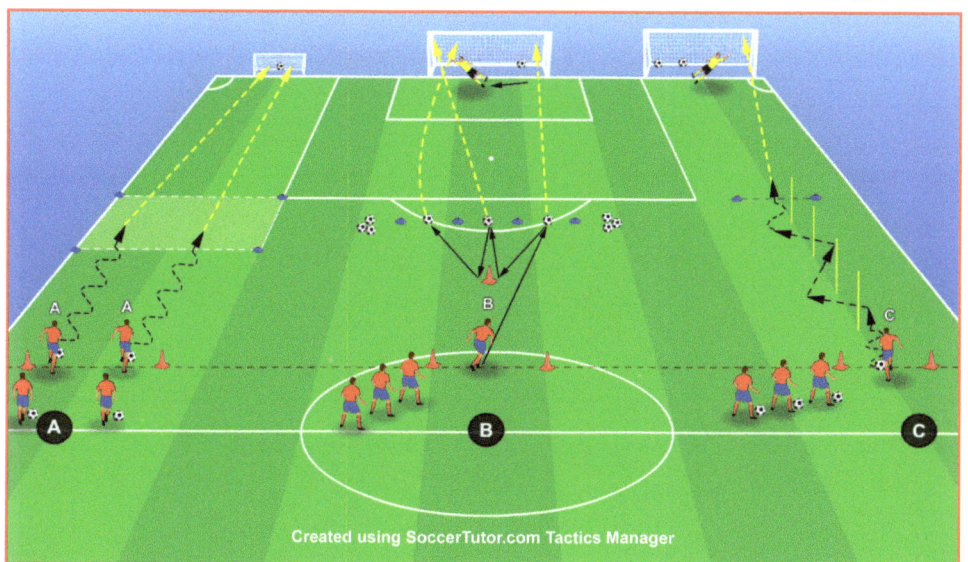

Objective: Dribbling, speed and shooting.

Description
Using half a youth pitch, we have 3 groups of 4 players, all starting from the cone gates as shown.

- A. This is a race and 2 players start at the same time and dribble forward. They must shoot into the small goal from within the highlighted area. Only the first goal scored counts.
- B. The player runs forward to the first ball and shoots. He then turns, runs back to the large red cone, and runs forward again to shoot the second ball. This is then repeated to shoot the third and final ball. At least one of the shots must be struck with the weaker foot.
- C. The player dribbles through the poles and through the blue cone gate. He then shoots at goal.

In each group, they count the goals scored. Rotate the groups after 3 minutes.

Progressions
1. All goals must be scored with the weaker foot.
2. Demand more speed in the execution.

Chapter 8: Finishing

Dribbling Exercises + Combined Finishing

2 x 4 min

Objective: Dribbling, turning and finishing.

Description

Using half a youth pitch, we have 3 groups of 3 players, all starting from the red cone gates as shown.

One player from each group starts with a ball at the same time:

A. Player A runs forward at speed, turns round the cone and dribbles into the box. Once through the blue cone gate, he shoots at goal.

B. Player B runs forward through the blue cone gate and shoots.

C. Player C zig-zags through the poles and dribbles through the 2 sets of blue cone gates. He then passes across for Player B to take a second shot.

They each move to the next group (A -> B -> C -> A) and the practice continues with the next players.

Progressions

1. Player A moves across to defend and try to block Player B's second shot from C's pass (this is shown by the black line marked 'A5').
2. Make the players perform specific finishes - Left foot, right foot, header.

Chapter 8: Finishing

Ball Over Head: Spin, Control, Dribble + Shoot

8-10 min

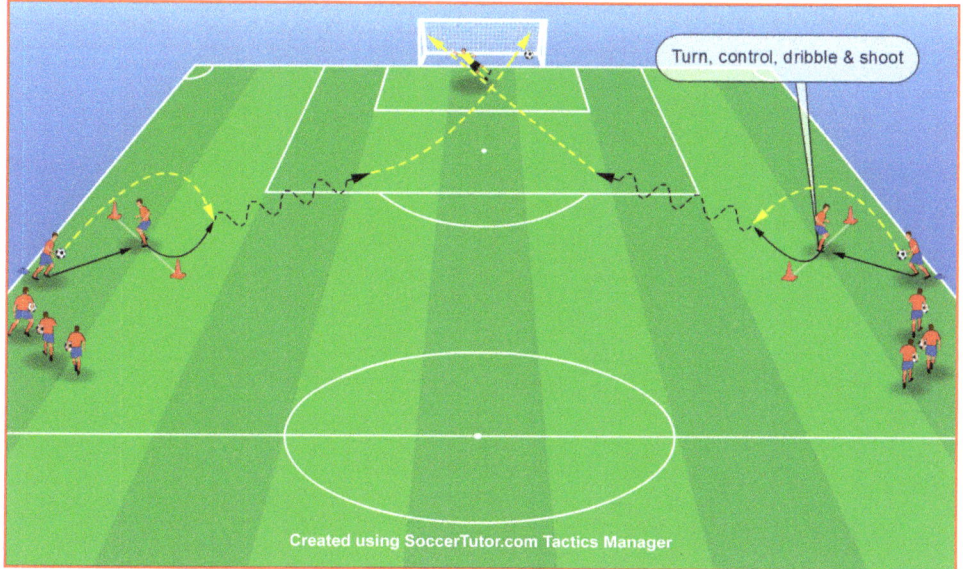

Objective: Receiving and shooting after a quick turn (spin).

Description

This is a simple practice. We have a cone gate on each side of the pitch in the positions shown. There is also a large goal with a goalkeeper.

One player (on both sides) stands in between the 2 cones without a ball. The first player with a ball throws it over his head and then moves forward to apply pressure.

The player spins (turns 180°), controls the ball, dribbles into the box and shoots.

The player who threw the ball moves in between the cones and the player who shoots moves to the other side of the pitch.

Variations

1. The players stay on one side and 2 teams compete. The first team to score 10 goals wins. You can then switch sides and repeat.
2. Change the throw to be at the player (not over him), so he must control and then turn.

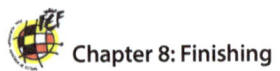

Chapter 8: Finishing

One-Two, Open Up, Receive + Shoot

8-10 min

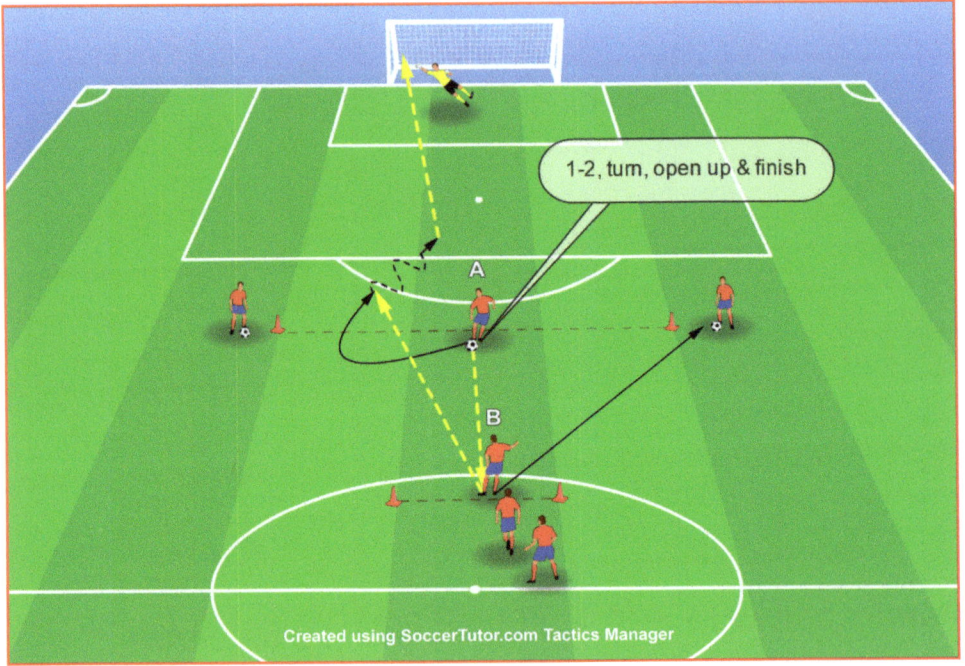

Objective: Opening up to receive and shooting.

Description

Using half a youth pitch, we mark out 4 cones in the positions shown.

We have a total of 6 players, with 2 players participating at a time. There is also a large goal with a goalkeeper.

Player A passes to B and makes a movement towards one side. Player B must read the movement and pass back (one-two) towards that side, within the cone gate. Player A opens up, receives on the half-turn, takes a touch into the box and shoots.

Player A collects his ball and moves to position B. Player B moves to position A.

Progressions

1. After passing, B applies pressure to make A's finish more difficult.
2. Place a ball in between the 2 cone gates. Once A has taken his shot, B collects this second ball - he dribbles forward and tries to score. Player A defends the goal.

Chapter 8: Finishing

Drop, Turn, Receive + Finish

8-10 min

Description

In this practice, 2 groups of players are positioned on either side of the goal. We also position 2 red poles outside the penalty area as shown. All players in both groups have a ball except for the first players (1) who start the practice.

1. The first players (1) run forward on the coach's whistle.
2. The second players (2) make a diagonal pass for the player in the other group.
3. The first player turns round the cone and moves forward to receive.
4. The first player receives and takes 1 or 2 touches into the penalty area.
5. He shoots at goal.

The player who shoots moves to the opposite side and the next players go in this continuous practice.

Variations

1. Change the position of the poles to vary the distance and angle of the shots.
2. All shots on the left side must be with the right foot / All shots on the right side must be with the left foot.

Chapter 8: Finishing

Sprint, Turn, Receive + Shoot in a Three Player Combination

8-10 min

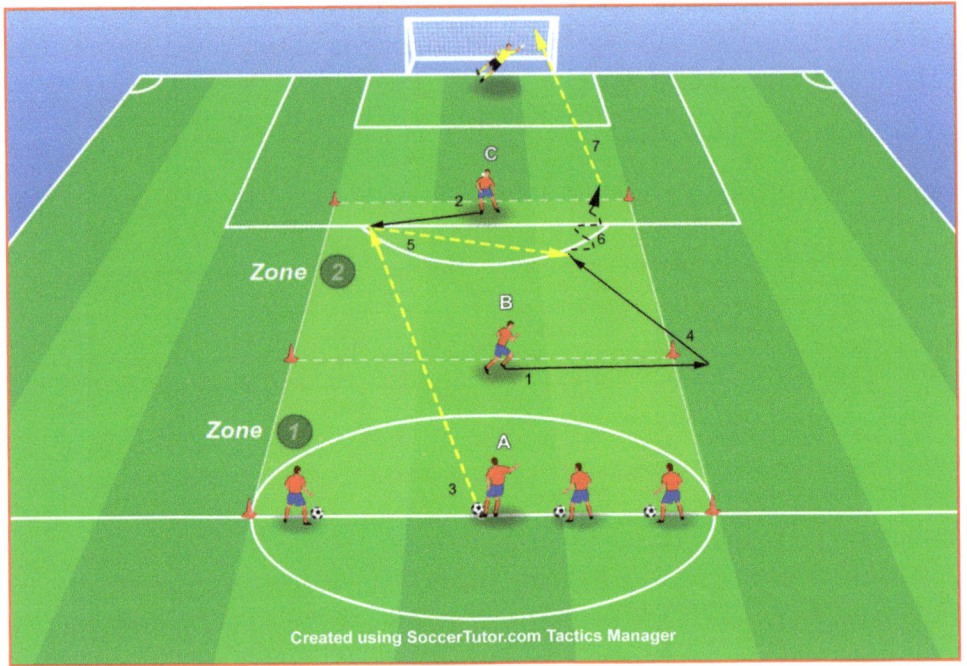

Description

Using half a youth pitch, we mark out the area shown with 2 zones. There is also a large goal with a goalkeeper. Player C starts at the top of zone 2, B starts at the end of the zone 1 and A starts from the beginning line.

1. B makes his first movement to either side.
2. C must read the movement and move in the opposite direction.
3. A passes to C.
4. B makes a second movement forward to receive the next pass.
5. C passes to B.
6. B controls the pass and enters the penalty area.
7. B shoots. The players move to the next position (A -> B -> C -> A).

Variations

1. Player C determines the place where he wants to receive the ball and makes the first movement. Player B must then react and run to the opposite side.
2. Player C receives the pass from A and tries to turn and shoot (B applies pressure).

Chapter 8: Finishing

Quick Combination, Supporting Run from Wide + Finish

8-10 min

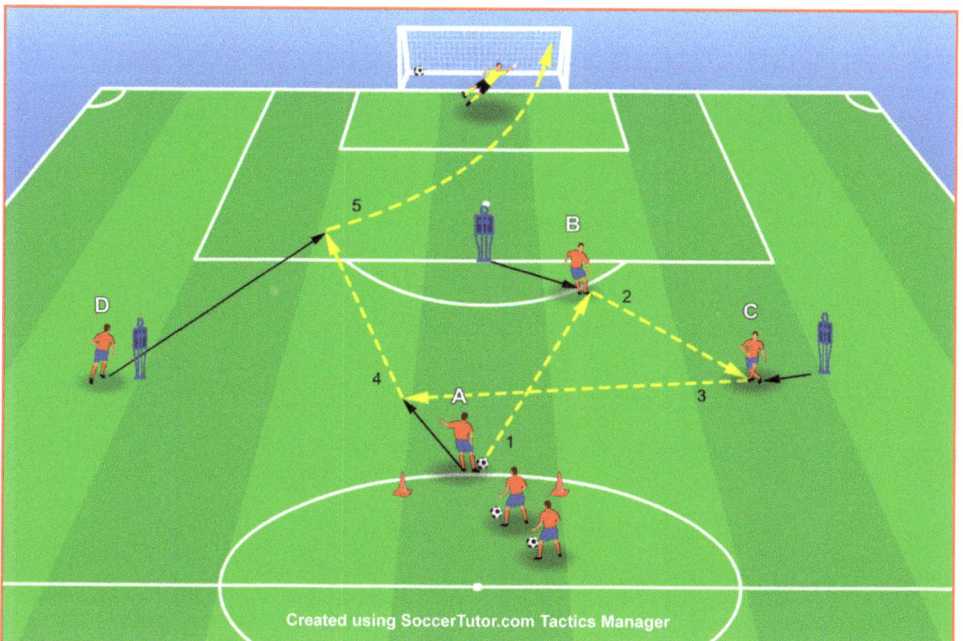

Description

Using half a youth pitch, we position 4 cones as shown. The combination includes 4 players, with 2 extra players waiting at the start position.

Player A starts with a pass to B who moves off the cone to pass back to C. Player C passes across A who moves forward.

Player D makes a forward diagonal run and A passes forward for D to run onto inside the penalty area. The sequence is concluded with D shooting at goal.

The players rotate positions (A -> B -> C -> D), with D collecting his ball and moving to the start.

After a set time, switch positions C and D so the players practice on both sides.

Variations

1. Have 2 groups going at once and count the amount of goals scored.
2. Change the scoring system, so that goals with the stronger foot are worth 1 point and goals with the weaker foot are worth 2 points.

Chapter 8: Finishing

Double One-Two and Finishing Practice

8-10 min

Objective: Quick one-two passing combinations and finishing.

Description

Using half a youth pitch, we have 2 groups of players performing the same sequence in different directions, as shown. We mark out 3 large cones on both sides (A, B & C) and we have a large goal with a goalkeeper at both ends.

The practice starts with Player A on both sides simultaneously. Player A plays two consecutive one-two combinations with B and C, who both move off their cones to pass back. After C's pass back, A shoots at goal.

Depending on the age/level of the players, they can use 2 or 3 touches. The players rotate positions (A -> B -> C -> A). After a set time, the 2 groups switch sides.

Variation: You can alternate the sequence of passes between the 3 players, as long as you maintain the premise of receiving on the move.

Progressions

1. You can have 2 balls running at the same time on each side.
2. Perform the entire practice with the players limited to 1 touch.

Chapter 8: Finishing

Short and Long Passing with Finishing from Cut Backs

8-10 min

Objective: Accurate passing, movement and finishing.

Description

Using half a youth pitch, we have 2 groups of players performing the same sequence in different directions simultaneously. We mark out 2 poles in the positions shown and we have a large goal with a goalkeeper at both ends.

One each side, there is a player waiting without a ball in the positions shown. The rest of the players have a ball each at the start position.

1. The first player passes to the inside player and makes a long run forward.
2. The inside player plays a deep pass (outside the poles) into the path of the first player, who receives and dribbles round the second pole.
3. The first player cuts the ball back into the centre.
4. The inside player from the group on the other side turns and shoots.
5. The first player becomes an inside player and the inside player moves to the start position on the other side. The practice is continuous.

Depending on the age/level of the players, decide how many touches the players are allowed for different elements of the practice. We try to progress to a stage where all the finishing is done with 1 touch.

Chapter 8: Finishing

Finishing in a 3 v 3 SSG with 2 Extra Attacking Outside Players

8-10 min

Objective: Quick attacks and finishing.

Description

In a 30 x 40 yard area, we split the pitch into 2 equal zones. We play a 3 v 3 small sided game with both teams having 2 extra outside players (1 on in each side in the attacking zone).

The practice starts from the goalkeeper and the aim is to attack quickly and score, using the advantage of the outside players. If a team scores directly from a pass by an outside player (as shown in the diagram), then the goal counts double.

The inside players are limited to 2 touches and the outside players have 1 touch.

You can play for 4 minutes and switch the inside and outside players. Alternatively, you can switch the players after a team scores 3/4 goals.

Variations

1. Goals with the weaker foot count as 2 goals.
2. Headed goals count as 3 goals.
3. Allow the 2 defending inside players to use their hands when defending.

CHAPTER 9

Attacking Combination Play

Chapter 9: Attacking Combination Play

ATTACKING COMBINATION PLAY TRAINING METHODOLOGY

- Attacking combinations can be practiced in many different ways - they can be done with players in different positions and with different numbers of players. In this chapter, we present different ways to practice attacking combinations.

- The key to successful attacking combinations is the timing of runs and the weight of the passes.

- We can practice attacking combinations with several balls, doing two, even three actions in a row, making the practices much more difficult.

- We present a variation of combinations and actions.

- Depending on the level of your players, you can adjust the practices. At the RFEF Coaching School, we progress from practices with low difficulty to practices with high difficulty throughout the season.

- The difficulty of the practices is determined by the speed of execution that we demand from the players.

Chapter 9: Attacking Combination Play

Quick One Touch Pass and Move Combination Practice

8-10 min

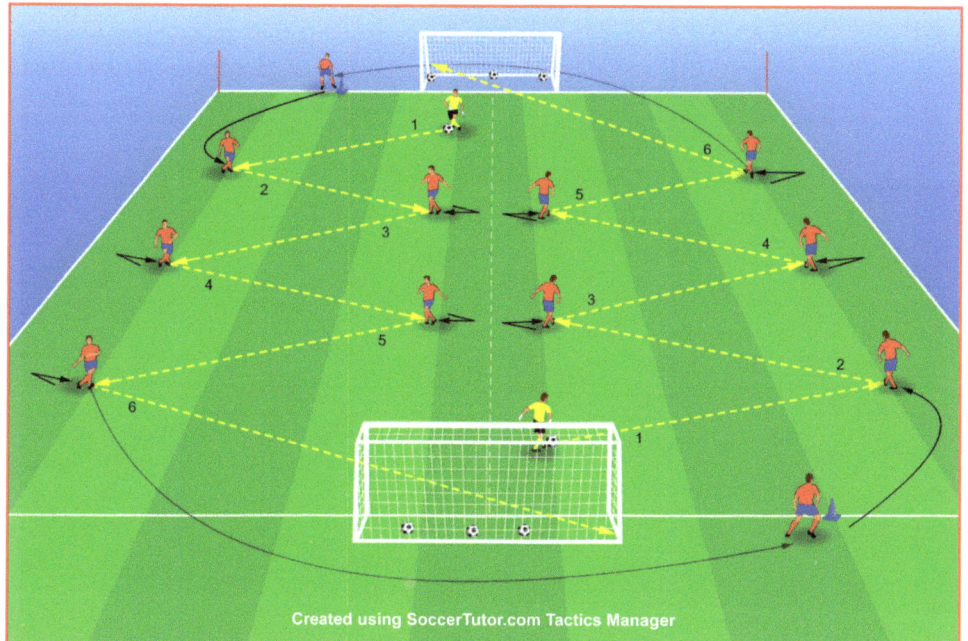

Description

Using an area suitable for the age/level of the players, we split the pitch into 2 equal zones with a large goal and goalkeeper at each end.

This is a continuous passing circuit with play starting from the 2 goalkeepers simultaneously. We have 1 goalkeeper and 5 players in the positions shown on each side. There is also 1 extra player waiting on each side next to the blue cone.

The goalkeeper starts with a diagonal pass to the first player - the diagonal passes continue as shown with the players using 1 touch, until the fifth player passes into the goal. He then runs around to join the other side.

All of the other players follow their pass and move to the next position - the goalkeeper gets a new ball and the player waiting moves to receive to start the same sequence again. The goalkeepers make sure to play their first pass at the same time.

Variations

1. To reduce the difficulty, you can let the players use 2 touches (control + pass).
2. The players stay in fixed positions and do not rotate (do not follow their passes).
3. Separate the 2 sides into 2 teams and see how many goals they score in a set time.

Chapter 9: Attacking Combination Play

Two Mirrored One Touch Combinations + Finishing

10 min

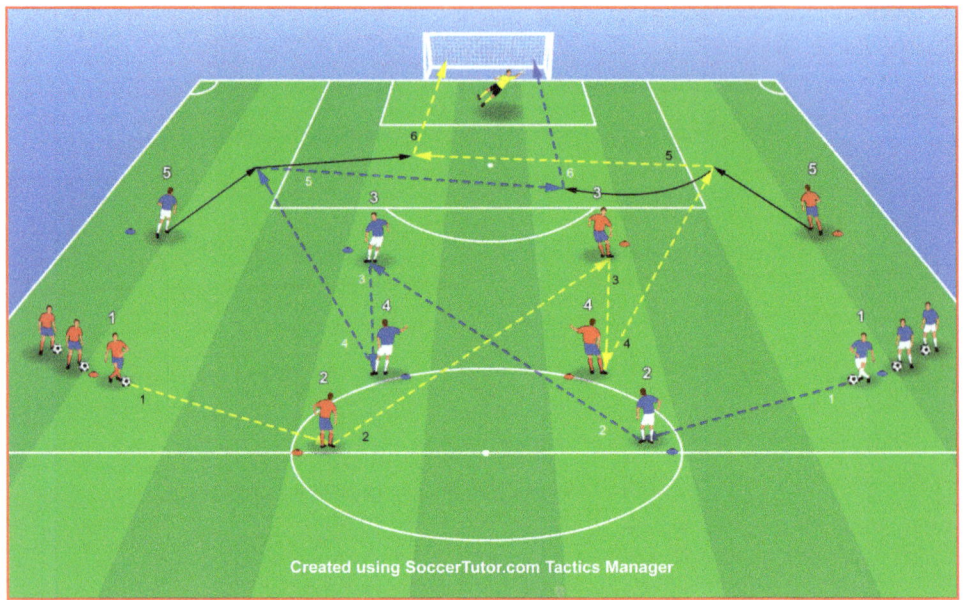

Objective: Fast one touch attacking combination play.

Description

Using half a youth pitch, we split the players into 2 groups and mark out 10 cones (5 for each group) in the positions shown.

The 2 groups start at the same time and play simultaneously - the players simply pass to the next cone (1-5) and then follow their pass.

The last pass to No.5 should be ahead of him so he can run onto it. When the blue No.5 receives, he passes across to the red No.5 to try and score past the goalkeeper, and vice versa. This is why it's important for the 2 groups to work at the same speed, so that they can combine at the end.

Depending on the level of the players, the next player can start after the 4th or 5th pass. After No.5 shoots, he collects his ball and goes to the start position.

Progressions

1. Add a defender in the penalty area to make scoring more difficult.
2. Player 3 can act as a defender after playing his pass back to Player 4.

Chapter 9: Attacking Combination Play

Quick Combination Play with Different Supporting Runs + Finishing

10 min

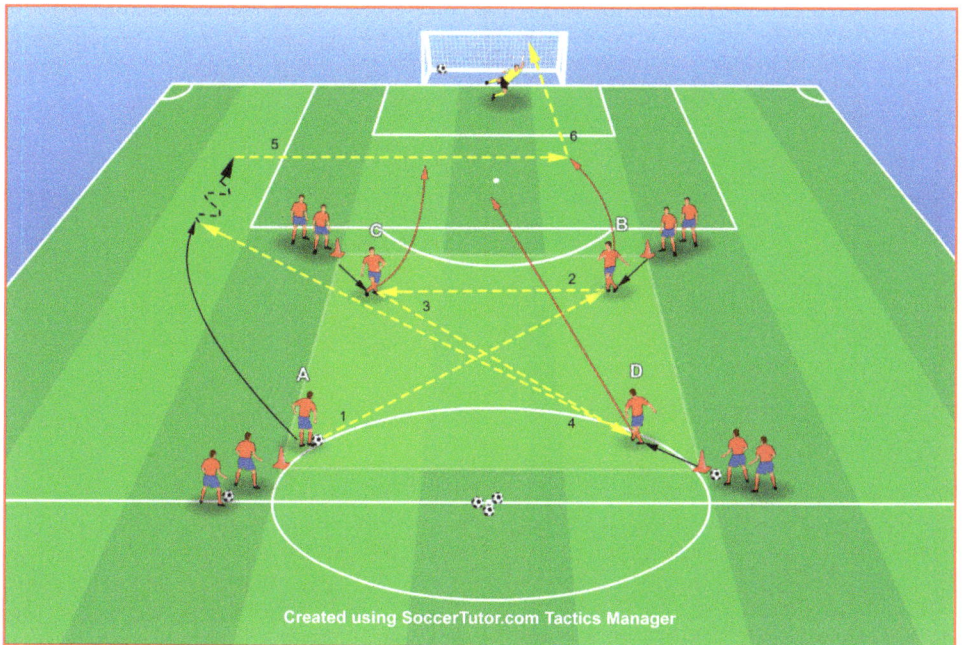

Description

Using half a youth pitch, we mark out 4 set positions with cones, as shown in the diagram. The players perform a specific passing sequence:

1. A starts with a diagonal pass to B. A also starts to make a movement wide.
2. B moves off the cone and passes inside to C.
3. C moves off the cone and passes back and diagonally to D.
4. D moves off the cone and plays a deep pass out wide for A to run onto.
5. A receives the pass and then passes/crosses into the penalty area.
6. B, C and D have all made runs into the box after their last pass, to try and score.
7. Players rotate to wait at the next position (A -> B -> C -> D -> A) and the next 4 players go.

Variations

1. Limit the number of touches.
2. Perform the sequence on the other sides, starting from the right side.

Chapter 9: Attacking Combination Play

Flank Play, Supporting Runs and Finishing

2 x 8 min

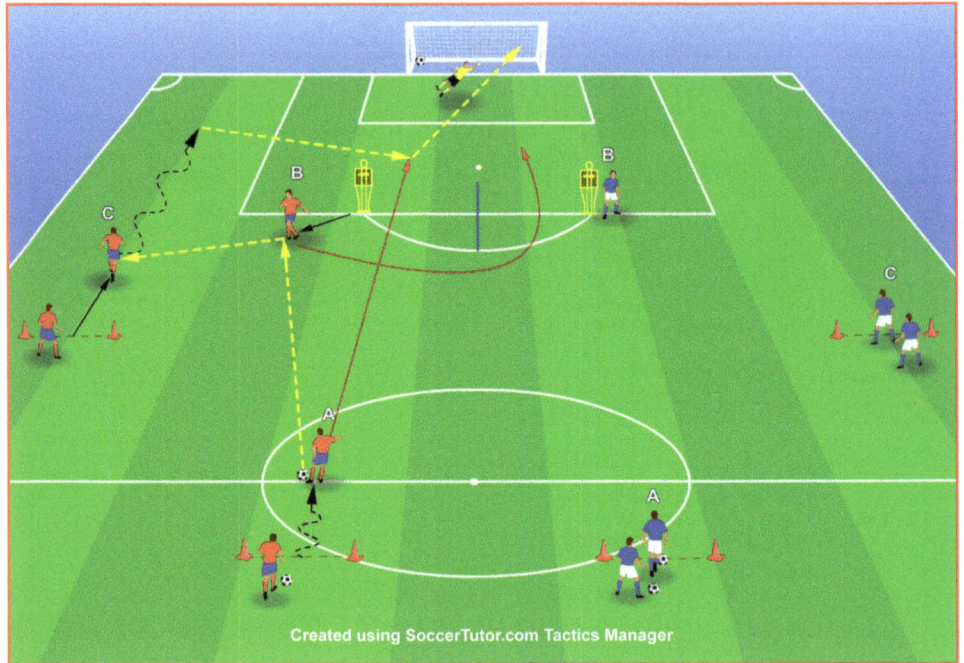

Description

Using half a youth pitch, we mark out 3 set positions on both sides, as shown in the diagram. The practice is performed on one side and then mirrored on the opposite side. This is a combination between 3 players.

1. The practice starts as A dribbles forward and passes to B who drops off of the mannequin. Player A then makes a run forward.

2. C moves forward and receives the lay-off from B. Player C dribbles forward and B makes a curved run around the pole and into the penalty area. By this time, A is also arriving.

3. C crosses/passes for either A or B to score past the goalkeeper.

The players rotate positions (A -> B -> C -> A). As soon as the players are finished on one side, the other side repeat the same sequence.

Progressions

1. Player B from the other side (blue) moves across to apply pressure on red B when he goes to receive, and vice versa on the other side.

2. The two sides compete against each other to see who can score the most goals.

Chapter 9: Attacking Combination Play

Pass High Up the Flank, Supporting Runs + Finishing

2 x 6 min

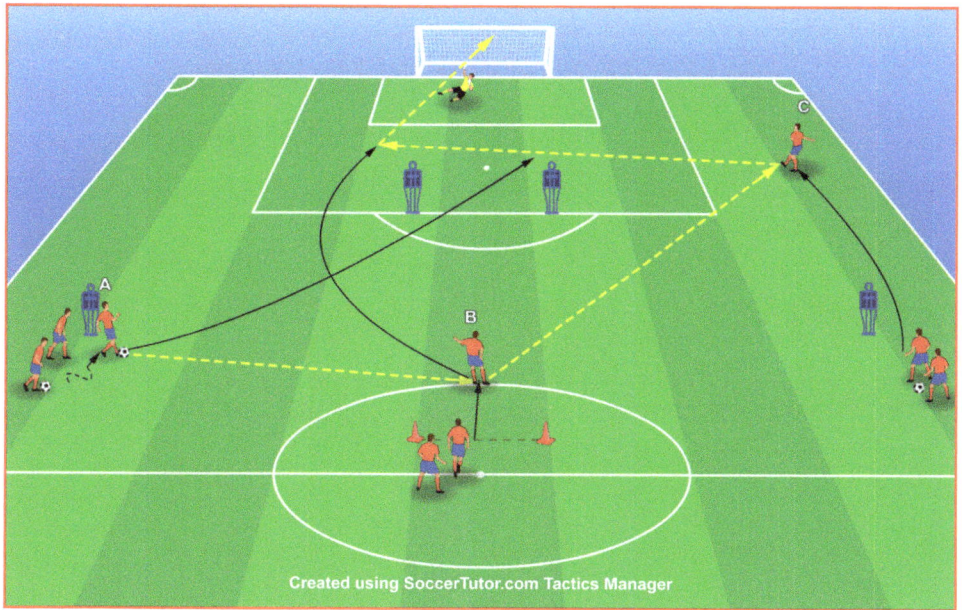

Objective: Switching play with supporting runs to finish.

Description

Using half a youth pitch, we mark out cones and mannequins as shown.

1. The practice starts with A passing inside to B who moves forward to receive. A starts his diagonal run forward.

2. C has made an advanced run up the flank and B passes to him. B makes a curved run into the penalty area.

3. C receives high up on the flank and crosses/passes for either A or B to score past the goalkeeper.

Each player moves to wait at the next position (A -> B -> C -> A), and the next players go. After 4-5 minutes, swap the A and C positions so the cross is made on the left side.

Variations

1. Add a defender in the penalty area to make scoring more difficult.
2. Vary the cross so that players have to finish using different methods - stronger foot along the ground, weaker foot along the ground, volley, header.

Spanish Football Federation Coaching

Chapter 9: Attacking Combination Play

Quick Combination Play to Receive High Up on Flank, Cross + Finish

8-10 min

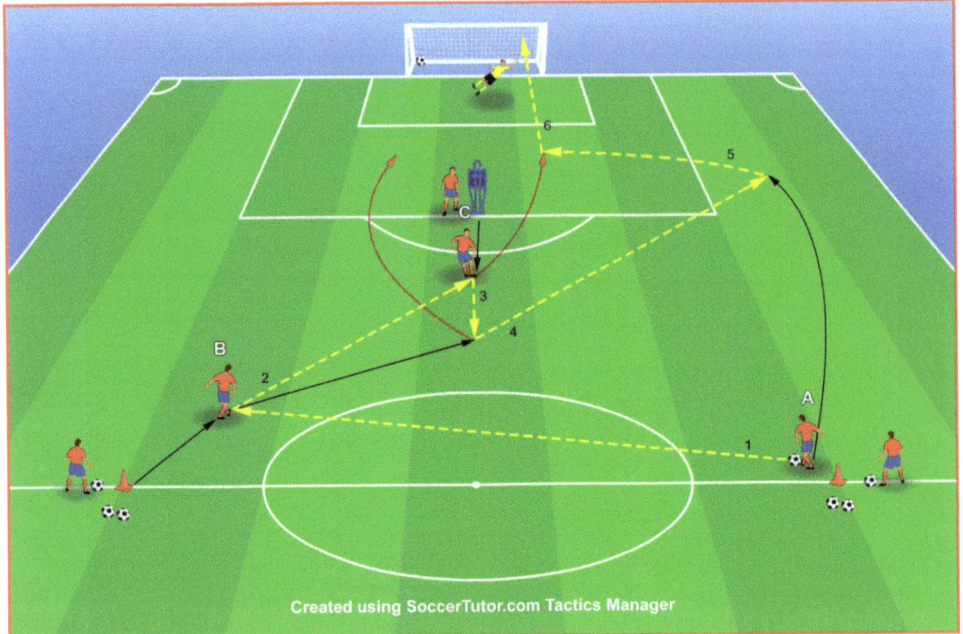

Objective: Attacking combination with forward's lay off and pass out wide

Description

Using half a youth pitch, we mark out 3 set positions, as shown in the diagram.

1. The practice starts with A passing to B who moves forward to receive. A starts to advance forward up the right flank.
2. C drops back and B passes to him. B moves forward and towards the centre.
3. C lays the ball off for B, who then passes out wide to A high up on the flank.
4. A crosses/passes the ball into the penalty area for B and C who make runs forward to try and score past the goalkeeper.

Each player moves to wait at the next position (A -> B -> C -> A), and the next players go. After 4-5 minutes, swap the A and B positions so the cross is made on the left side.

Progressions

1. Add an active defender in the penalty area to increase the difficulty.
2. The goal only counts if the player scores with a 1 touch finish.

Chapter 9: Attacking Combination Play

Quick Combination Play with Inside Movement to Receive + Shoot

8-10 min

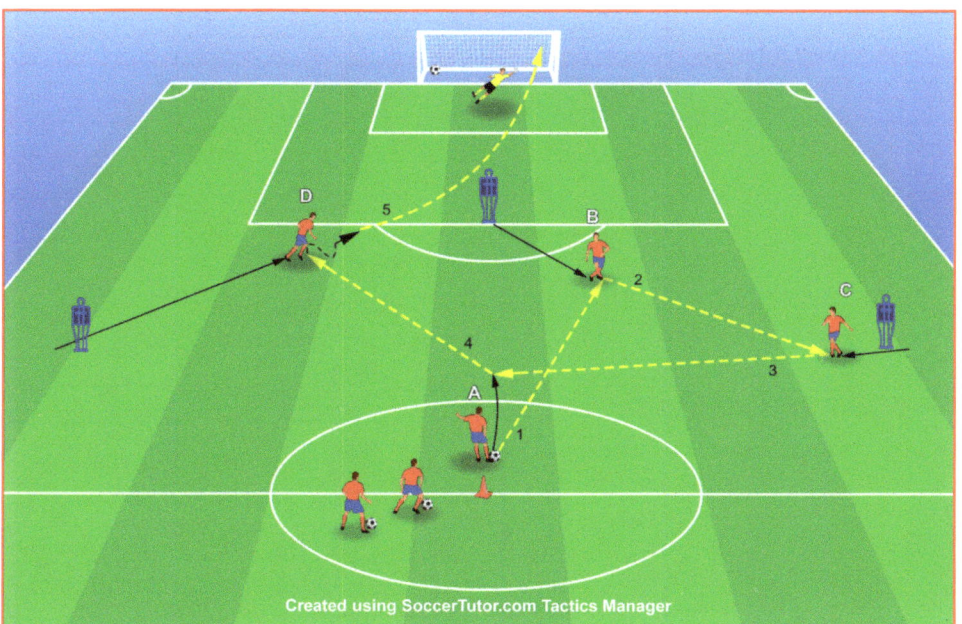

Description

Using half a youth pitch, we mark out 4 set positions as shown in the diagram. The players perform a specific passing sequence:

1. B drops off at an angle in either direction. In this example, B drops off towards the right side of the pitch, so A must pass to this same side.
2. B passes back to the player on that side (C) who moves inside off the mannequin.
3. C passes inside and in front of A, who moves forward.
4. D moves off his cone and makes an advanced run. A passes to D so he can receive on the move.
5. D controls the ball and shoots, trying to score past the goalkeeper.

If B had dropped off to the left side of the pitch, he would pass back to D. D would pass inside to A and the final pass would be from A to C on the right side. Each player moves to the next position (A -> B -> C -> D -> Start), and the next player A starts.

Variations

1. Make it a competition with 2 teams alternating - the team with most goals wins.
2. Change the scoring system, so that a goal scored with the stronger foot is worth 1 point and a goal scored with the weaker foot is worth 2 points.

Chapter 9: Attacking Combination Play

Quick Combination Play with Fast Support, Cross + Finish

8-10 min

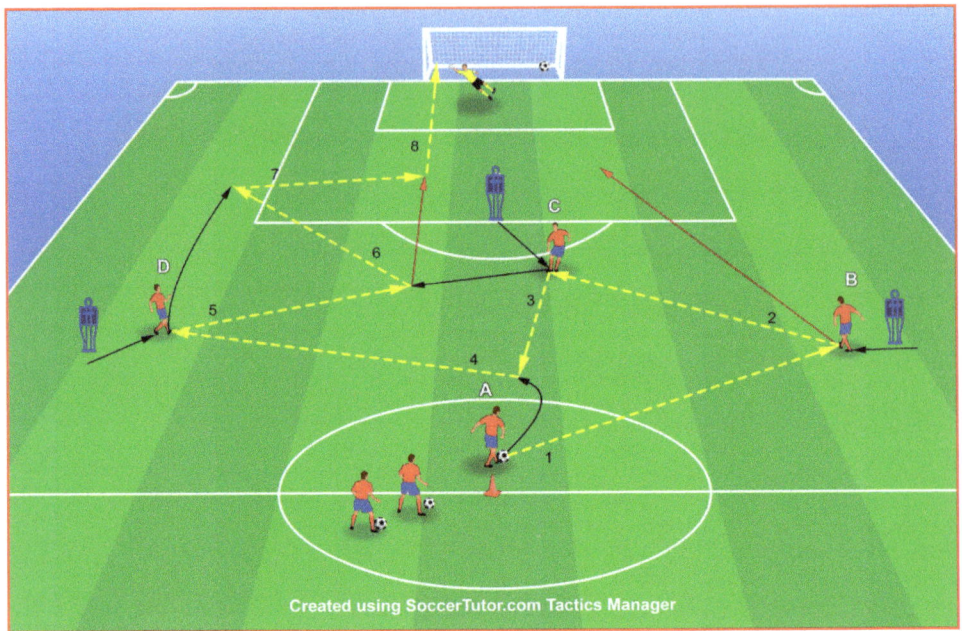

Description

Using half a youth pitch, we mark out 4 set positions as shown in the diagram. The players perform a specific passing sequence:

1. C drops off at an angle in either direction. In this example, C drops off towards the right side of the pitch. As C makes a movement towards the right side of the pitch, A must pass to B who is on that side.
2. B passes to C.
3. C lays the ball off to A who moves forward.
4. A passes to the left side for D who moves off the cone.
5. D plays a one-two with C who moves across. He then passes/crosses into the box for B and C who time runs into the box, trying to score past the goalkeeper.

If C had moved to the left side of the pitch, the first pass would be from A to D and the final combination play would be between C and B on the right side. Each player moves to the next position (A -> B -> C -> D -> Start), and the next player A starts.

Progressions

1. Make it a competition with 2 teams alternating - the team with most goals wins.
2. Score with stronger foot = 1 point, weaker foot = 2 points, header = 3 points.

Chapter 9: Attacking Combination Play

Combination Play to Receive on the Flank, Cross + Finish

10-15 min

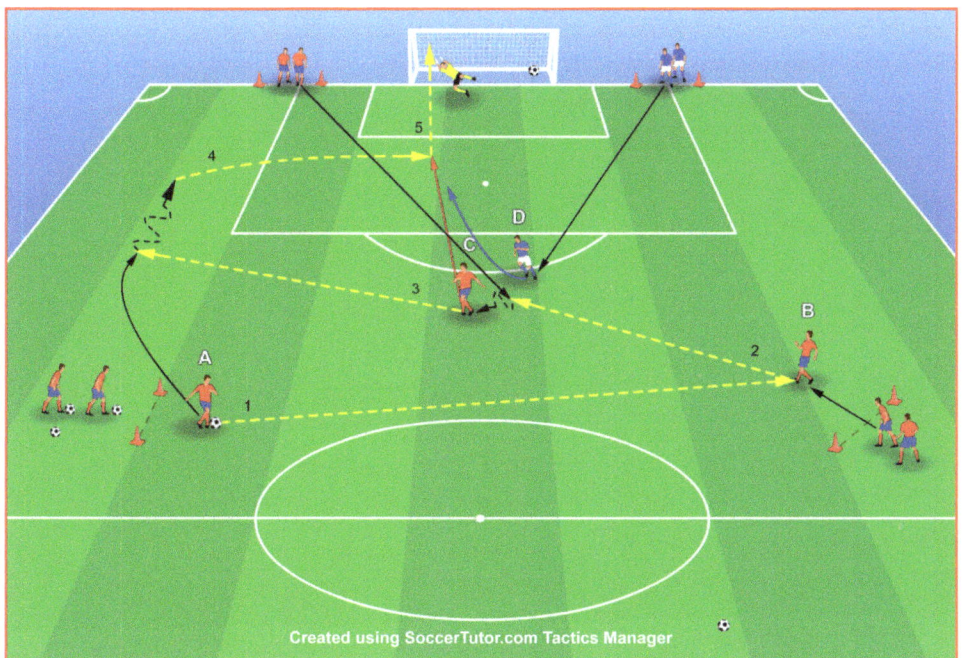

Objective: Attacking combination with a supporting run and finish.

Description

Within half a youth pitch, we use cones to mark 4 different start positions for A, B, C and D (defender). In each position we have 3 players as shown.

1. A passes across to B who moves forward. A then makes a run out wide. Players C and D run forward as shown.

2. B passes to C who has dropped to receive. D (defender) provides passive defence.

3. C must demonstrate good technique to receive the ball and then play a controlled pass for A to run onto.

4. A controls the ball on the move and crosses/passes the ball for C to finish. The defender (D) is fully active and tries to prevent or block the final shot.

Each player moves to wait at the next position (A -> B -> C -> D -> A), and the next players go.

After 5-6 minutes, swap the A and B positions so the cross is made on the right side.

Spanish Football Federation Coaching

Chapter 9: Attacking Combination Play

Win the Ball (2 v 4) in the Centre and Counter Attack Combination

15 min

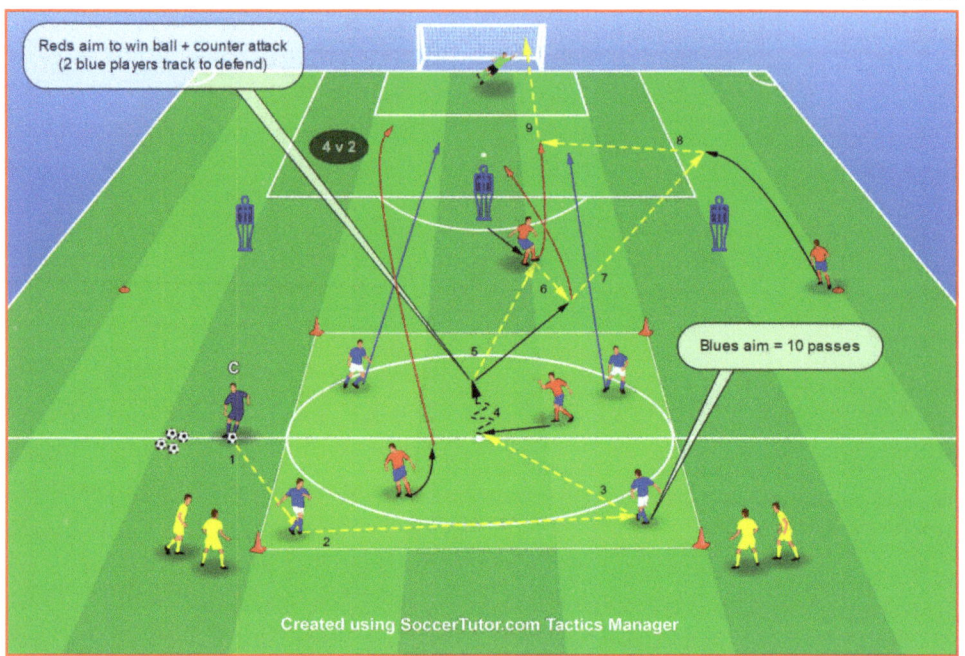

Description

We have 3 teams of 4 players (2 teams play at a time). We mark out an area in the centre and have 3 mannequins in the positions shown, who represent defenders.

1. The practice starts with the coach's pass and the blue team try to complete 10 consecutive passes (1 point) within the area with a 4 v 2 numerical advantage.

2. If the reds win the ball, they start a counter attack by passing to the forward who moves to receive. There is also a wide player on one of the sides.

3. Both red players move forward to join the counter attack and 2 blue players track back to defend. If the reds score, they get 1 point. The other 2 blue players remain in the central area.

After this phase is concluded, the reds now move to wait outside the central area. The coach passes to the yellow team who move inside.

We again have a 4 v 2 situation - the yellows try to complete 10 passes.

The blues try to win the ball and counter attack - their other 2 players are now waiting in advanced positions (one forward and one wide player who can be on either side).

Variation: Limit players in the central area to 2 touches, making it more likely they lose the ball.

©SoccerTutor.com *Spanish Football Federation Coaching*

CHAPTER 10

Tactical Development

TACTICAL DEVELOPMENT TRAINING METHODOLOGY

- For this age group, tactical development is all about the actions in which the team becomes aware, to play the game they want to play in competition.

- At the RFEF Coaching School, we focus on building up play from the back, mainly along the ground using good passing combinations.

- We play 8 v 8 with this age group and we use a 3-3-1 formation, which we feel best develops our training methods and game model.

- For the younger players, we make the practices simpler for the attacking team. We either have big numerical advantages for the attacking team or we have defenders that hold hands - this builds confidence in the players and they are able to gain more touches, more passes in training.

Chapter 10: Tactical Development

Build Up to Finish in an 8 v 2 Zonal Game

8-10 min

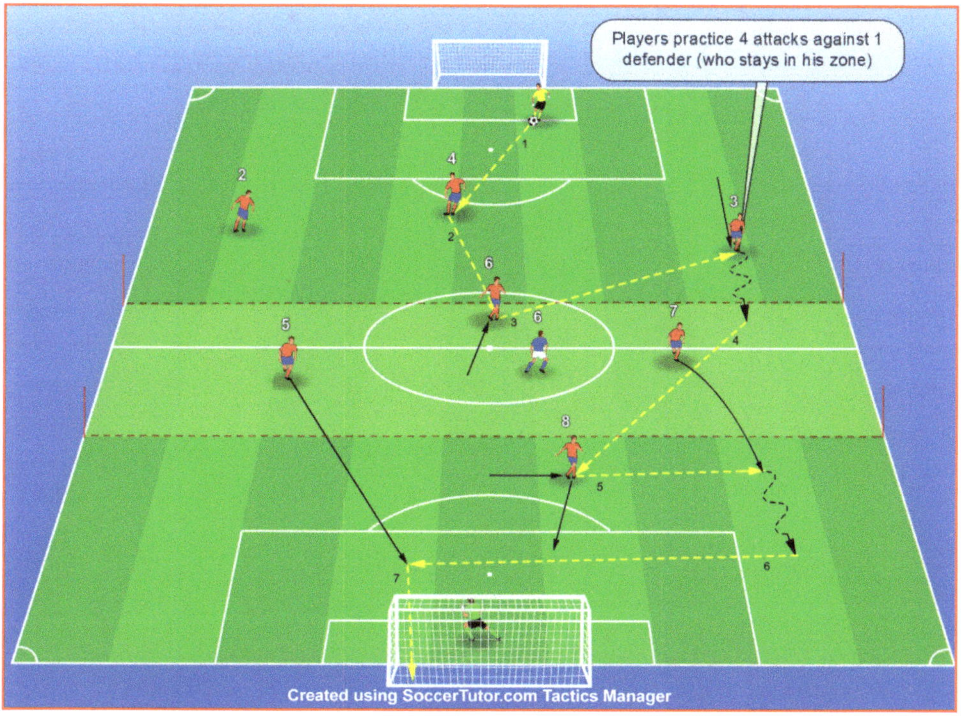

We use a youth pitch which is approximately 50 x 65 yards (45 x 60 metres)

Objective: Building up play and attacking within a set 3-3-1 formation.

Description

For these practices (4 more to follow), we use our 3-3-1 formation. The pitch is split into 3 zones as shown, with a middle zone marked out.

We have 1 opposition midfielder (blue No.6) who defends within this zone and cannot leave it. You can rotate this player after each phase is completed.

The red team build up play and attack. Using our game system and passing along the ground, the red team carry out 4 attacks. Each time the practice starts from the goalkeeper. The goals are counted and once the 4 attacks are over, the blue team will play against 1 red midfielder - this way there is a winner at the end.

Variation

The coach calls out a number (1-3) which represents a specific pattern the players must then use for their attack.

©SoccerTutor.com   Spanish Football Federation Coaching

Chapter 10: Tactical Development

Build Up to Finish in an 8 v 3 Zonal Game + Quick Transition

8-10 min

We use a youth pitch which is approximately 50 x 65 yards (45 x 60 metres)

Objective: Building up play and attacking within a set 3-3-1 formation + the quick transitions from attack to defence.

Description

This is a progression of the previous practice. We now have 2 zones marked out - there is a blue midfielder in one zone (No.6) and a blue defender (No.4) in the other.

If a blue player is able to win the ball and pass to his teammate, the attack is deemed to be finished. However, if the reds win the ball back before this happens, they can then continue their attack.

The rest of the aims and rules remain the same as the previous practice.

Variations

1. The coach calls out a number (1-3) which represents a specific pattern the players must then use for their attack.
2. Start the practice with different game situations e.g. A throw-in, the opposition have just won the ball in the middle etc.

Chapter 10: Tactical Development

Build Up to Finish in an 8 v 4 Zonal Game

8-10 min

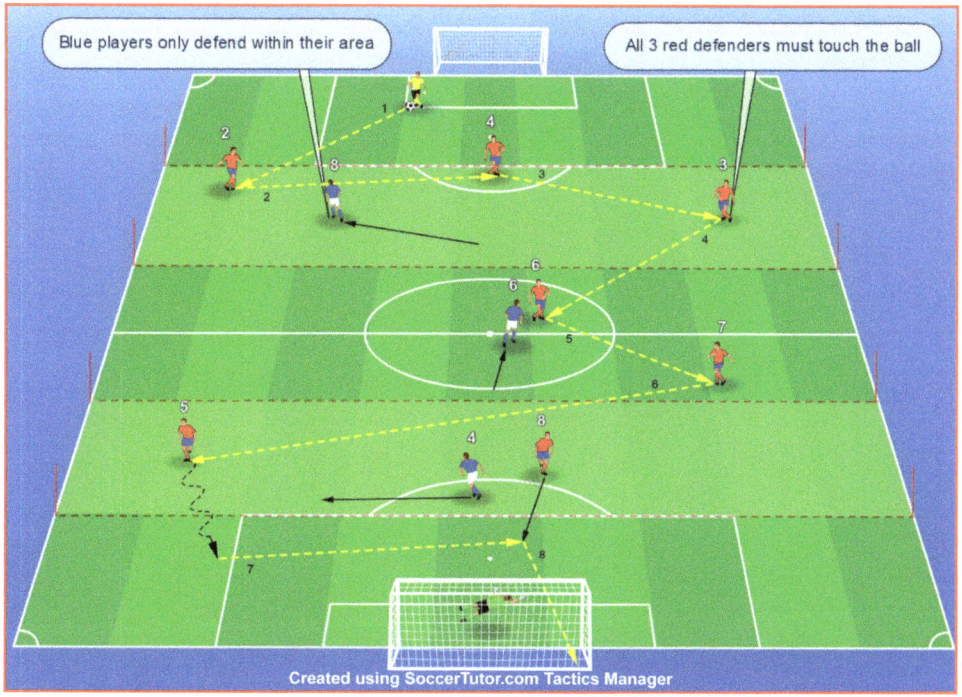

* *We use a youth pitch which is approximately 50 x 65 yards (45 x 60 metres)*

Description

This is a progression of the previous practice. We now have an extra zone where a blue forward (No.8) is added to put pressure on the red defenders when building up.

If a blue player is able to win the ball and pass to his teammate (or shoot), the attack is deemed to be finished. However, if the reds win the ball back before this happens, they can then continue their attack.

The rest of the aims and rules remain the same as the previous practice.

Variations

1. The coach calls out a number (1-3) which represents a specific pattern the players must then use for their attack.
2. Start the practice with different game situations e.g. A throw-in, the opposition have just won the ball in the middle etc.

Chapter 10: Tactical Development

Build Up to Finish in an 8 v 8 Zonal Game with Restricted Defenders

8-10 min

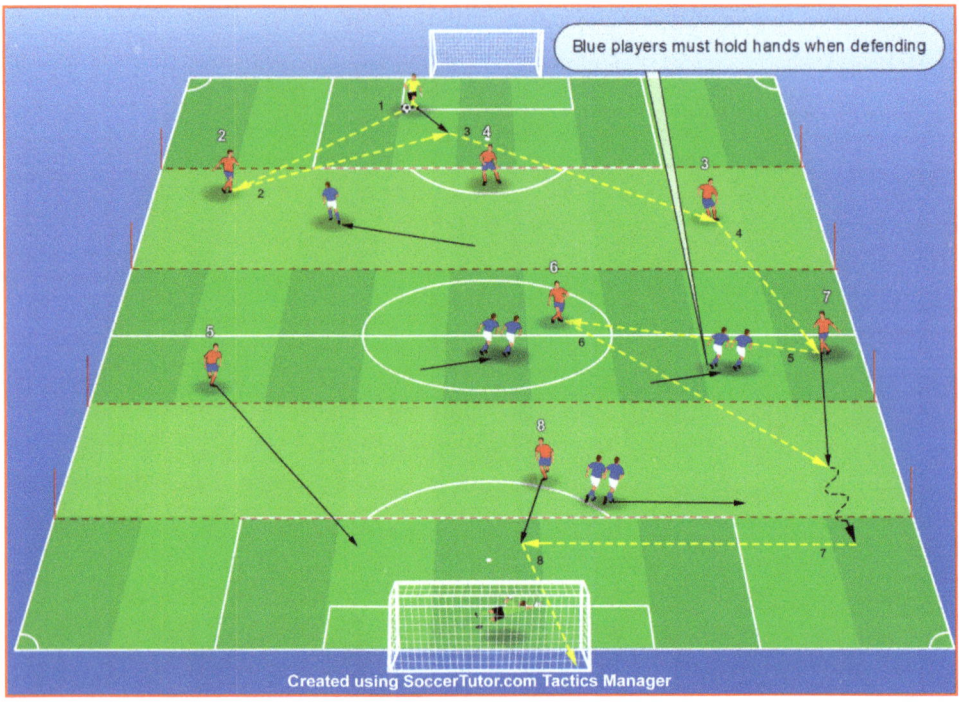

We use a youth pitch which is approximately 50 x 65 yards (45 x 60 metres)

Description

This is a progression of the previous practice. We still have 1 blue forward, but now we have 2 blue pairs holding hands in the midfield zone and 1 blue pair holding hands in their defensive zone.

Now if the blues win the ball, the attack is deemed to be over. The rest of the aims and rules remain the same as the previous practice.

Variations

1. The reds have 2 opportunities to score. If they do, they get to attack 2 more times. If they don't, then the blue team become the attacking team.
2. Start the practice with different game situations e.g. A throw-in, the opposition have just won the ball in the middle etc.

Chapter 10: Tactical Development

Build Up to Finish in an 8 v 8 Small Sided Game

8-10 min

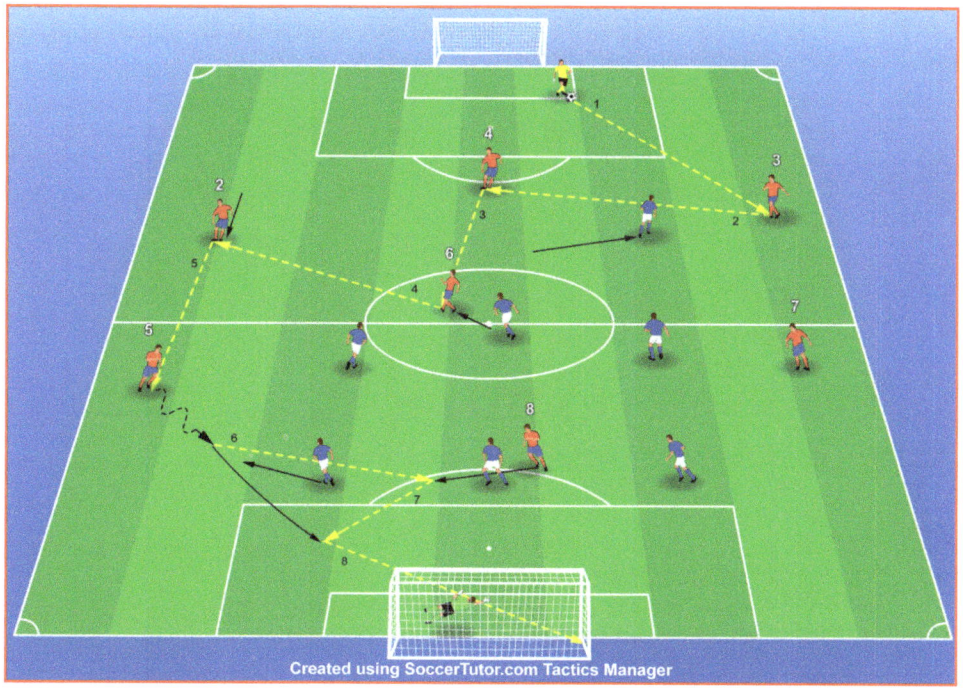

* *We use a youth pitch which is approximately 50 x 65 yards (45 x 60 metres)*

Objective: Building up play and attacking with full resistance in an 8 v 8 game.

Description

In this progression and final practice of the chapter, we now play a normal 8 v 8 game without zones. The practice starts from the goalkeeper.

The coach sets out specific rules for the attacking team. Here are some examples:

1. For a goal to count, the ball must be touched by all 3 defenders (as shown in the diagram).
2. For a goal to count, the ball must be touched by 2 defenders, 2 midfielders and the forward.
3. Every player must touch the ball for a goal to count.

If the team manages to score, they get 1 point and start a new attack. If they don't score, the game starts again with the opposition's goalkeeper.

©SoccerTutor.com Spanish Football Federation Coaching

CHAPTER 11

Circuits

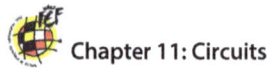

Chapter 11: Circuits

CIRCUIT TRAINING METHODOLOGY

- In this chapter, we show you a few circuits that we do regularly at the RFEF Coaching School.

- We use circuits to introduce players to speed and agility exercises, using equipment such as hurdles and speed rings.

- In these circuits, there is always work with a ball as well, whether it be dribbling elements or duels/finishing.

Chapter 11: Circuits

Dribbling Circuit with Different Techniques and Turns

2 x 3 min

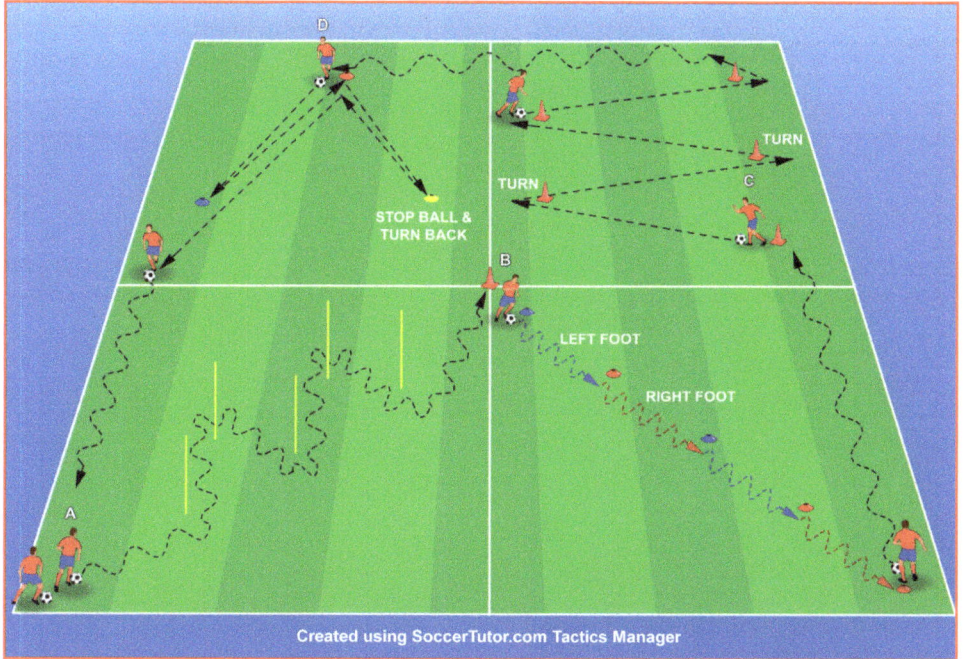

Objective: Ball mastery/dribbling with both feet and control with turns.

Description

For this practice, we mark out 4 x 10 yard squares and the players perform different dribbling elements in a circuit (A -> D), as shown.

a. Slalom through the poles using the insides of both feet.

b. Dribble alongside the cones, using the left foot only from the blue cone to the red, and right foot only from the red cone to the blue.

c. Dribble at speed, changing direction sharply round each cone.

d. Dribble to first cone, stop the ball with sole and dribble back to first cone - repeat with the second cone and dribble back to the start.

Progressions

1. Put the cones/poles closer to each other to increase difficulty.
2. Increase the total distances and amount of cones.
3. Increase the tempo at which the players must dribble with the ball.

Chapter 11: Circuits

2 v 2 Possession Game + Speed & Agility Exercises with Finishing

10 min

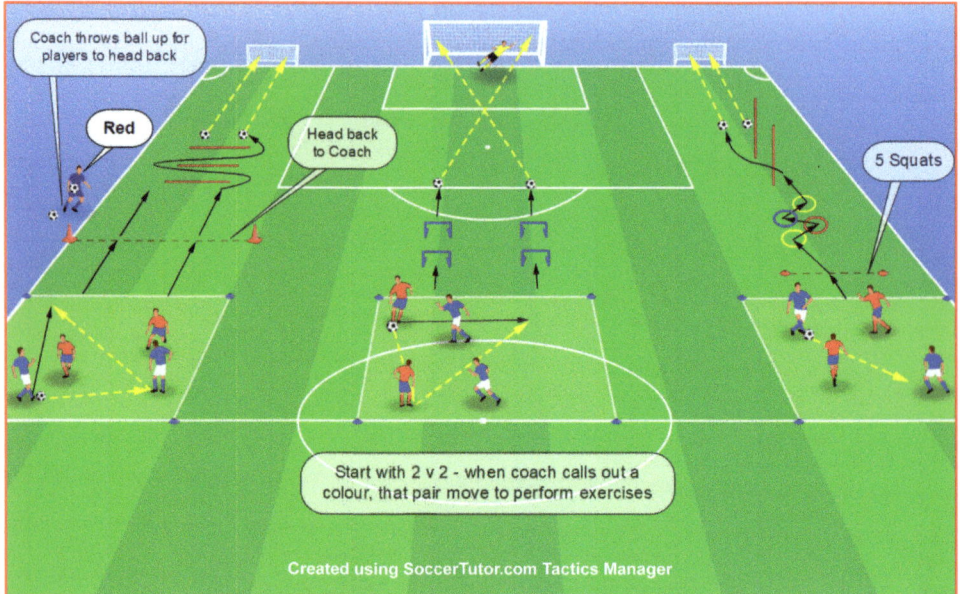

Objective: Speed, strength, agility, possession play and finishing.

Description

Using half a youth pitch, we divide the players into 3 groups with 2 blue players and 2 red players in each.

All 3 groups start by playing a 2 v 2 possession games in the areas shown. They wait until the coach calls out a colour. When the coach calls a colour (red in diagram example), those 2 players run to perform the following exercises:

1. Run to the line - the coach throws a ball up and the players head it back into his hands. The players perform the speed exercise round the poles (or cones) with lateral movement, and finish by scoring in the small goal.

2. Run forward, jump over both low hurdles, sprint to ball and shoot.

3. Run to the line and perform 5 squats, then perform the speed exercise using the speed rings (side-to-side landing with 1 leg). Finally, slalom through the poles and score in the small goal.

After completing the speed & agility exercises, the players then move to the next group and the practice continues in the same way.

Chapter 11: Circuits

Speed & Agility Circuit Training with Finishing (3 v 1 Attack)

8-10 min

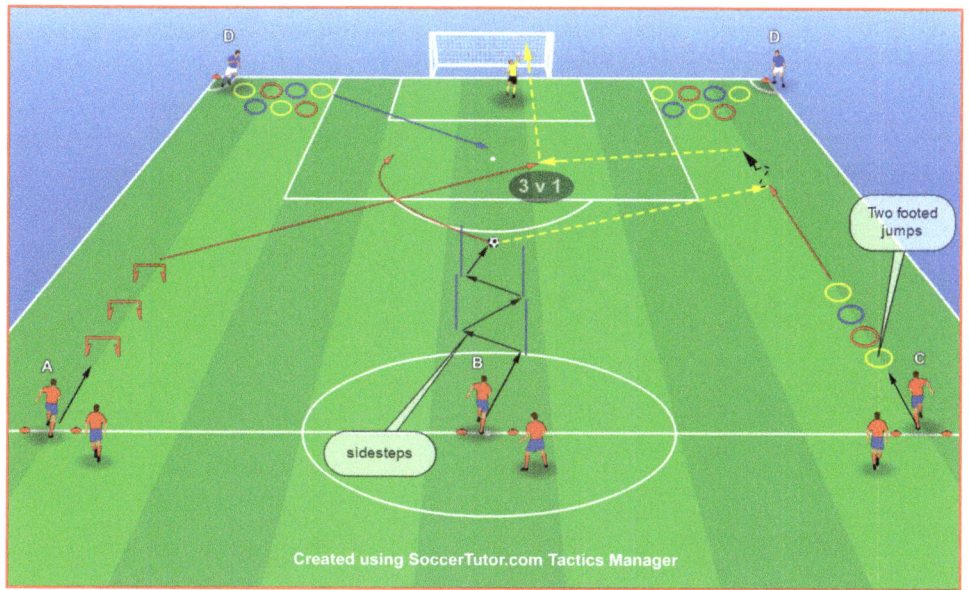

Objective: Speed, strength, agility, passing and finishing.

Description

Using half a youth pitch, we have 4 stations (A-D) as shown. Each player performs their exercise before taking part in the 3 v 1 attack:

A. Jump over 3 low hurdles and then make a run into the penalty area.

B. The player sidesteps his way through the poles, collects the ball and passes out wide for Player C to run onto.

C. Jump through the speed rings (landing on two feet inside each ring), sprint forward to receive the pass from Player B and cross/pass for either A or B inside the penalty area.

D. Lateral movements through the speed rings (landing with 1 foot alternately) and then sprint into the centre of the penalty area to defend the attack.

A and B try to score and D tries to stop them. After the attack finishes, all of the players move to the next station (A -> B -> C -> D -> A), and the next players waiting go.

Chapter 11: Circuits

Speed & Agility Circuit Training with 3 v 2 Duel

20 min

Objective: Speed, agility and attacking in a 3 v 2 situation.

Description

Using half a youth pitch, we mark out 5 different circuits for 5 different players:

1. A1: Runs forward, jumps over all 3 low hurdles, collects the ball and tries to score.
2. A2: Performs 5 squats and then slaloms through the poles.
3. A3: Sprints from cone to cone as shown, collects the ball and dribbles through the poles (slalom).
4. B1: Performs speed exercise round poles (or cones) with lateral movement, runs to the large cone and passes the ball into the small goal.
5. B2: Performs speed exercise using the speed rings (side-to-side, landing with 1 leg).

After each player has completed their circuit, A3 dribbles his ball forward to launch a fast 3 v 2 attack against the 2 blue players.

You can have the 2 teams compete - if a goal is scored, the reds win a point and if not, the blues win a point, or rotate the player positions (A1 -> A2 -> A3 -> B1 -> B2).

THANK YOU

First of all, I would like to mention the positivity of the RFEF. Since the first moment that we raised the possibility of doing this book, they have shown their full support for the project.

Thank you to Lolo Escobar, my right hand, Rodolfo Urías, Pedro Martínez, Manuel Barba, Fran Garrido, Jorge Broto and Carlos Sánchez ... who are all responsible for this book, my thanks and gratitude. We have tried to produce a high quality book and present the practices that we perform most during the season with our players. Also, thank you to all the coaches at the RFEF Coaching School and Foundation, as since being with them we have enriched ourselves.

Thank you to the Royal Spanish Football Federation, the president, Ángel María Villar for his opportunity and for his words, and to all of its members for the opportunity they have given me to make this book. To Vicente del Bosque and to all those that I have crossed paths with in football and have helped me to this day. You have made me stronger and I have learnt so much in the last few years. This range of experience is how I was able to produce this book.

Finally, I want to dedicate it to my whole family, my first club (Aldapeta CD) to my brothers, my father, my wife, Noelia, my children, Nahia and Edu txiki, to Gaspar Rossety who in glory is one of my great propellers, to Juan Luis Larrea, for his unconditional support, to Jorge Perez for believing in me without hardly knowing me, to Enrique Vedia, one of the key inspirations in my life. But also to the one who has always instilled in me that "Do not stop trying and try it if you believe in it" ... To my mother, rest in peace, she always bet on me and thought that I would get everything I have today. FROM MY HEART, THANK YOU.

Eduardo Valcárcel

FREE TRIAL

Football Coaching Specialists Since 2001

TACTICS MANAGER
Create your own Practices, Tactics & Plan Sessions!

www.SoccerTutor.com/TacticsManager
info@soccertutor.com

PC   Mac   soon!   soon!   soon!

www.ingramcontent.com/pod-product-compliance
Lightning Source LLC
Chambersburg PA
CBHW061253230426
43665CB00026B/2921